BLITZ DIARY

BLITZ DIARY

LIFE UNDER FIRE IN WORLD WAR II

CAROL HARRIS

First published 2010

The History Press
The Mill, Brimscombe Port
Stroud, Gloucestershire, GL5 2QG
www.thehistorypress.co.uk

British Library Cataloguing in Publication Data.
A catalogue record for this book is available from the British Library.

ISBN 978 0 7524 5172 5

Typesetting and origination by The History Press
Printed in Great Britain
Manufacturing managed by Jellyfish Print Solutions Ltd

CONTENTS

1

PREPARING FOR WAR

The Second World War would be a war in which civilian populations across Europe would be primary targets. As such, two factors dominated Britain's preparation for the European war that seemed increasingly likely as the 1930s progressed: aerial warfare and the use of poison gas. Planning focused on civil defence, a term used more and more throughout that decade.

Airships and, later, aeroplanes had dropped bombs on civilian populations across the country during the First World War, killing over 1,400 people in just over 100 raids. The technology of aerial flight in particular had advanced dramatically in the twenty years since the end of that conflict. This would have an impact on military tactics as aeroplanes travelling at high speed replaced airships.

In 1924, the British government set up the Committee for Imperial Defence, which established an ARP (Air Raid Precautions) subcommittee to look at 'the organisation for war, including Civil Defence, home defence, censorship and emergency war legislation'. This subcommittee met secretly for nine years, discussing ways of warning the population of air raids, preventing damage through such measures as restricting lighting (the blackout), gas masks, repairing damage and dealing with casualties.

In 1933, the year Hitler became Chancellor of Germany, the subcommittee set out detailed plans for ARP services to

Pictured by the family Anderson shelter, these two still carry their gas masks which suggests it is early in the war. Anderson shelters consisted of curved sheets of aluminium buried several feet into the ground. Earth was shovelled on the top of the shelter – ideally deep enough to plant flowers and vegetables.

be organised through local authorities. By 1935, when the ARP Department of the Home Office was set up, these local authorities had been briefed on their responsibilities: the scheme would mean forming services to provide first aid, to deal with poison gas attacks and to rescue civilians caught in air raids. In that year, Hitler announced that Germany would re-establish her air force and introduce military conscription – both of which were in contravention of the Treaty of Versailles, which ended the First World War.

The first official broadcast on ARP services went out in January 1937 on the BBC. Debate had raged for some time as to the appropriate response to the threat of air raids. Some felt that the introduction of such a scheme was itself provocative. In the *British Medical Journal*, doctors argued whether they should co-operate at all. Across the country local authorities reflected this ambivalence. Some services were well organised with volunteers training to deal with the effects; most were not. In general, ARP was regarded as something of a joke.

Attitudes changed markedly in 1937, when cinemas' newsreels showed the impact of the aerial bombardment of the Basque town of Guernica during the Spanish Civil War. Guernica was attacked on 26 April of that year by the German and Italian air forces in support of the fascist or nationalist side. Dr Duncan Leys' letter to the *British Medical Journal*, written a few weeks later, sums up the feeling that Britain was woefully unprepared for the onslaught that was to come:

22nd May 1937
SIR, – It is no longer correct, I find, to think of our work as one of healing. I learn from the Home Office Instructor on Air Raid Precautions in the Birmingham area that my duties in the next war are to aid the police in 'preventing panic,' to 'reassure' the gas casualties, 'to get it into people's heads that whether they have gas-proofed rooms or not the important

thing is for them to be under cover in their own houses,' that 'the whole danger of gas attacks lies in the lowering of national morale,' and that the medical profession, as a group of persons 'who can speak with authority,' is to maintain that morale, in which function the Home Office considers them of only less importance than the police.

These actual quotations from a lecture are no misrepresentation of the general tenor. Having heard pacificists [sic] maintain that the main object of the Government's air raid precautions scheme was a military one that is, to make panic or any mass protest against the continuation of war less likely, and that protection from death and injury in air raids on cities was only possible by the erection of bomb-proof shelters which the Government considered too expensive to contemplate – I attended this official lecture, delivered by a doctor to other doctors, on the invitation of the British Medical Association in order to learn what attitude was taken by the Home Office officials themselves. I was prepared to hear the lecturer say that, with the Prime Minister, he acknowledged that nothing like protection to a city population was possible short of bomb-proof and gas-proof shelters constructed for the purpose, but that until the Government had made its plans, the possibility of sudden air attack on cities existed, and that the Air Raid Precautions Department offered some advice as better than none, that a few lives might be saved by such advice, and that he was there to tell us how we could help in this limited sense. Such an approach to the question would have had my full sympathy and co-operation.

The lecturer opened by assuring us that he had no connexion with the fighting services: the Air Raid Precautions Department 'had nothing warlike about it,' and was intended 'purely for the passive protection of the civil population.' He told us that it would require anything from a few inches to several feet of concrete to protect buildings from air raids, and that 'nobody had suggested that it was possible to protect the whole population in this way.' He went on to describe how we might advise people to erect on scaffolding three layers of filled sandbags on their roofs, with two feet interval between the layers, to protect them from splinters from high explosives. No enemy, he continued, would use gas bombs only; high explosives would first be used to demolish important centres like railway stations, public buildings – including hospitals, which would become too dangerous to be used for other purposes than as casualty clearing stations – and generally to do as much damage to structure as possible. Thermite bombs would follow in thousands with the aim of starting a general conflagration in the city beyond the powers of the fire brigades to deal with. Gas would next be sent down by spray or bomb, and it was then that doctors and first-aid services would be needed to 'prevent panic,' to 'reassure' those affected, and to persuade people to remain in their houses.

A passing mention was made of the difficulties of protecting the aged and children and invalids, but respirators 'were a second line of defence' and the main thing was that people should stay indoors. No mention was made of the impossibility for most working-class families of providing a room for gas-proofing (a room rendered uninhabitable because of boarded windows and blocked ventilators or chimney), and although the lecturer said that the modern bombing plane could aim accurately to within seventy-five yards no mention was made of the certainty that windows and gas-proofing would certainly be destroyed over a wide area surrounding the fall of a high-explosive torpedo.

No opportunity was given for questions or discussion, and one is therefore unable to say how far the audience of some thirty doctors accepted the role indicated to them of persuading their neighbours that the Air Raid Precautions Scheme could really save them and their children when it must be perfectly obvious to the meanest intelligence that it can do nothing of the sort, and that the whole apparatus of the scheme is designed to deceive people into thinking that it will. I am not accusing the lecturer of deception: he was painfully honest. It is obviously much more satisfactory, from a military point of view, that people should die quietly in their homes than that they should run about the streets and possibly mob Cabinet Ministers: they might even, fearing retaliation, try to persuade our own airmen from their efforts to destroy French, German, Italian, or Russian cities.

But I should judge that the audience was almost entirely uncritical, accepting war as inevitable and their duty that outlined by the lecturer. The lecturer, by the way, inadvertently said these will be your duties, but corrected himself, and hoped we might avoid seeing the actuality.

I put it to one member of the audience after the lecture that we were being asked to perform a military duty and to help deceive people into thinking that protection was possible on the lines proposed in order that mass protest against war should be made less likely. His reply was that if an enemy attacked us in this way we might as well make it possible for our Air Force to do the same to his cities.

I should personally be sympathetic to any Government which, if it thought that the risk of war could not be avoided, sought power to tax the people to the utmost limit to provide them with protection, putting the facts in an unvarnished way before them and placing the responsibility upon them. But I hold that our people have the democratic right of deciding for themselves, now, in time of peace, whether modern warfare can justify itself, by having none of the facts hidden from them. I call the Government's Air

> Raid Precautions Scheme wilful deception of the people. I believe also that it is a deception which will defeat its own object. Panic is a mild word for the wrath which the people, rudely enlightened by the first English Guernica, will display against their rulers and officials when they survey the ruins and the dead.
>
> I am, etc.,
>
> DUNCAN LEYS, M.D.Oxon.

The British government passed the ARP Act, which came into effect on 1 January 1938. This actually compelled local authorities to set up ARP schemes and offered substantial funding towards the costs of doing so. Schemes had to include wardens, first aid, gas decontamination, casualty clearing stations and repair and demolition services. The Auxiliary Fire Service, representing a major expansion of the established fire brigades, was also introduced.

In September 1938 Germany threatened Czechoslovakia and it seemed that war was imminent. The Munich Agreement, Prime Minister Neville Chamberlain's attempt to bring 'peace in our time', was welcomed by cheering crowds for Britain. Hitler assured Chamberlain and the rest of Europe that he had no further territorial demands. In return, Britain and France ignored the Czech government's views and agreed to Germany incorporating into its own borders the Czech Sudetenland. But a massive increase in volunteers for the various civil defence schemes, in the year between Munich and the outbreak of war in September 1939, suggests that few believed this to be anything more than a delay in which to prepare as fast as they could for the onslaught.

Shelters were dug in public parks, people filled sandbags and buckets of water, and Anderson shelters were distributed to civilian homes. Public meetings, volunteer recruitment drives and training schemes for civil defence personnel and the general public gathered pace. Expectations were that the air raids would start soon after war was declared and would result in planes dropping poison gas on the major cities of Britain. Official estimates, based on the effects of bombing in Spain, were that 120,000 people would die in the first week of the war, and about twice that number would be injured. This estimated total of 360,000 casualties in one week was in fact more than twice the number of people killed and injured in Britain in this way during the whole of the war.

Ann Maxtone Graham was the American wife of a British serviceman living in Earl's Court, London. This is her memoir, written initially to give her family in America an idea of the war in Britain:

> Little by little, we started to check what we should do if war came, for we began to believe it might. In March of 1938, Pat enlisted in the 151st battery anti-aircraft brigade and I bought six gallons of gasoline which I stored in a funny little summer house in the back garden. At one time it housed the boys' rabbits. I bought a can of ether in case I had to put the dogs and cats to sleep.
>
> Trenches were dug in Kensington Gardens and Hyde Park and sand bags made protective walls round doorways. Our war didn't burst upon us like Pearl Harbor. It came in sneaky little ways. Suddenly there was a flier in the mail box: 'Notice to inhabitants – Air Raid Precautions.' Gas masks would be issued, they said 'should it become necessary.'
>
> Pat was away in camp for two week's training and came home on September 26th but was called up the next day, and off he went to his guns and rockets.

Ann volunteered to deliver gas masks to people who could not leave their homes: 'I went flying around, had an hour's training in how to fit the horrid things and then set off on my delivery route.' While she was out on her rounds:

> There was a group of people huddled around a wireless and they beckoned me to join them. Mr Chamberlain had just arrived home from Berlin and a conference with Hitler. He was shouting 'Peace in our time! Peace in our time! All is well.'
>
> We all collapsed like pricked balloons. After all, he was the Prime Minister, and we thought he knew what he was talking about. I crept home, had my hot bath, but a stiff drink instead of my cup of tea. It had been quite a day. Pat came home from his gun site and went back to his job. There were certain evenings and weekends given to training. Life went on as usual but there were stirrings, and we felt that maybe someone was doing a little pushing and trying to get ready in case war really came.
>
> It occurred to me that if other people were doing a little pushing, maybe I should do a little quiet pushing too. So I went up to the Town Hall of Kensington, and after a little struggle, I got in to see the man who was in charge of the First Aid Posts.

As a result, she set up a depot at her home making surgical dressings:

> I don't know how many hundreds of thousands of dressings and bandages we made for Kensington, but when they were done they were all dispatched to the Town Hall. To our fury, they were never acknowledged nor did we receive one word of thanks. I know they were used, for some of our friends saw them in the First Aid Posts and recognised my writing on the labels.
>
> So much for Kensington! We supplied Hackney with the things and they were gratefully acknowledged.

We rented a house in the New Forest for a month at Christmas time (1938). It was right on the Solent opposite the Isle of Wight and all the big ocean liners went past on their way to Southampton. Although we didn't know it, this was our last peaceful Christmas for some very long years, and the last one that I would have with our children. Perhaps there was something that gave us a warning, as we made the most of it, kept the house full of guests, and didn't go back until the 21st January. British children get a month's holiday at Christmas.

My darling Dad died on 23rd March, and I longed to go home to Mother. She had a very nice niece staying with her and she begged me not to come. So I kept on with my surgical dressings and other odd jobs which came my way. A letter from my mother in May asked, 'Aren't you worried about the war? You never mention it, except for the surgical dressings.'

So I broke down and told her about the cans of gasoline stored in the summer house and the ether to put my dogs and cats to sleep if the need arose. No sooner had the letter reached Mother than I had a cable from her to say that she was coming to England at once. And so she did. I don't think she liked the trenches in the park or all the sandbags any better than we did. Nor did she like Pat going off to camp and leaving me all alone in London. She was so distressed about all this that at last I said the boys and I would go back to America with her for a visit. We sailed on July 22nd on the Georgic.

That is how I came to be in America when the war started. If I hadn't been there, I would never have sent the boys [Peter aged 12 and twins John and Michael aged 10] to America, as many of my friends and relatives did. But as I was there with them, I had to make a decision as to what I should do. I left them and, sometimes, I wish with all my heart that I had not.

Henry Beckingham, aged 19, had volunteered for military service in May 1939. He had just left technical college and started his first job as a draughtsman with a firm of consulting engineers:

> The decision was whether I should go for the TA [Territorial Army], spending weekends in the drill hall plus a 14-day camp annually, or alternatively to wait until the age of 20 years and spend 12 months away with the militia.
>
> I decided that the Territorial Army offered me the best option, as this would not seriously affect my civilian career. How wrong that decision was would be made very clear in the months ahead.

In addition to the call for volunteers to work in military and civilian services, a limited form of conscription was introduced in spring 1939. Under the Military Training Act, single men aged 20–22 were liable to be 'called up' for military training. They were to be known as 'militiamen' as they were not part of the regular army. At the outbreak of war the National Service (Armed Forces) Act extended conscription: men between the ages of 18 and 41 could now be compelled to serve in the armed forces.

R.H. Lloyd-Jones was another volunteer. He was a 29-year-old solicitor in Ealing when he joined the Territorial Army in 1938. He served first with the 424 AA (Anti-Aircraft) Company, 36 Searchlight Regiment, RE (Royal Engineers) and here recalls his experience of the first batch of conscripts:

> Spring and Summer 1939
>
> War was becoming very near and the Government had decided that the Anti-Aircraft defence would have to be permanently manned.
>
> Conscription had come into force and some of the first intake, the militia-men, as they were called, were being

trained for AA work, but until they were ready, the existing AA units like our own would have to man the sites, four weeks at a time. This process, quaintly named 'couverture', would start in the middle of June. Our regiment was one of those which were given the second period of four weeks, from 16th July to 14th August 1939 ... At about the same time we were told where our war sites would be. They were dotted over the country every few miles between Bedford and St Neots.

Some of us who had seen the posters 'Join the Anti-Aircraft and defend your homes' had not expected to be so far from our homes. It was explained to us that we would be in the outermost ring of the defences of London.

By now we were being sorted out according to the duties we would be carrying out on site.

Perhaps at this point I should mention that a Searchlight Detachment consisted of ten men who were numbered 1 to 10, these numbers signifying what they had been trained for, no 1 being the Detachment Commander. Nos 2 and 3 were spotters who watched for aircraft with binoculars, or more often with the naked eye because there were not enough binoculars to go round.

No 4 was the Projector Controller who stood or walked at the end of a bracket called the 'long arm' attached to the projector, with a kind of steering wheel to obtain (it was hoped) the right elevation of the beam. No 5 was an electrician, the searchlight operator, responsible for the arc lamp which produced the light. No 6 was in charge of the sound locator and was the Second in Command of the detachment. A one-way telephone enabled him to give directional orders to no 4 who wore a head set for this purpose. Nos 7 and 8 were the listeners who operated the Sound Locator, one of them listening in bearing and the other in elevation. No 9 was in charge of the lorry or diesel generator and No 10 was the spare man, which in actual fact meant that he was the cook.

Our training for these duties was partly individual, the spotters for instance being instructed in classes for aircraft recognition etc., and partly in Detachments comprising numbers 1 to 8 when we carried out imaginary engagements of 'targets' (as the aircraft was always known to us) with standard drill known as a 'manning drill' which always seemed to follow the same pattern, starting with 'target heard' and so to 'target seen' after which there was a crescendo of imaginary activities which always culminated in 'station attacked by low-flying aircraft – machine gun action' followed by the alarming order 'GAS' but eventually subsiding to 'target inaudible' and 'dowse'.

During the couverture we would be subject to Army discipline and apparently this made it necessary that the Army Act should be read to us. This was done on a parade outside the barracks one evening.

Captain Ingram did the actual reading and although he started in daylight, it went on so long, with section after section being read out, each one ending with the appropriate penalty which in nearly every case seemed to be death, that after a time the daylight failed and a sergeant had to stand by him with an electric torch.

There must have been four hundred men on parade. All of them had made sacrifices to join the Territorial Army and some of them would lose their lives in the impending war. These men stood there, motionless in the darkness while the voice droned on and on, threatening them with the death penalty. This made a very encouraging impression on me. While such things can happen, I said to myself, England will never lose a war.

Barrage balloons were dangerous and unwieldy, being on average 8.9 metres long and 7.6 metres in diameter. They were filled partially with hydrogen, partially with air, and were winched up usually from lorries and held in place by cables. Barrage balloons were essential defences against air attack as they forced all aircraft to fly higher around key areas such as industries, ports, towns and cities. This made bombers less accurate and forced them up into the range of anti-aircraft guns.

2

THE FIRST DAYS

Most of those old enough to remember the declaration of war on Sunday 3 September 1939 heard Neville Chamberlain's broadcast on BBC radio at 11 o'clock in the morning and remember the events that followed. The crisis was precipitated when Germany invaded Poland, and at a tense and angry sitting of the House of Commons on the Saturday evening, many MPs had voiced their objections to further appeasement. As his broadcast made clear, Chamberlain himself hoped war could be averted as it had been a year before.

> I am speaking to you from the Cabinet Room at 10 Downing Street.
>
> This morning the British Ambassador in Berlin handed the German Government a final note stating that, unless we hear from them by 11 o'clock that they were prepared at once to withdraw their troops from Poland, a state of war would exist between us. I have to tell you now that no such undertaking has been received, and that consequently this country is at war with Germany.
>
> You can imagine what a bitter blow it is to me that all my long struggle to win peace has failed. Yet I cannot believe that there is anything more or anything different that I could have done and that would have been more successful.
>
> Up to the very last it would have been quite possible to have arranged a peaceful and honourable settlement

between Germany and Poland, but Hitler would not have it. He had evidently made up his mind to attack Poland, whatever happened, and although he now says he put forward reasonable proposals which were rejected by the Poles, that is not a true statement.

The proposals were never shown to the Poles, nor to us, and though they were announced in a German broadcast on Thursday night, Hitler did not wait to hear comments on them but ordered his troops to cross the Polish frontier the next morning.

His action shows convincingly that there is no chance of expecting that this man will ever give up his practice of using force to gain his will. He can only be stopped by force.

We and France are today, in fulfilment of our obligations, going to the aid of Poland, who is so bravely resisting this wicked and unprovoked attack upon her people. We have a clear conscience – we have done all that any country could do to establish peace.

The situation in which no word given by Germany's ruler could be trusted, and no people or country could feel itself safe, has become intolerable. And now that we have resolved to finish it I know that you will play your part with calmness and courage.

At such a moment as this the assurances of support which we have received from the Empire are a source of profound encouragement to us.

When I have finished speaking, certain detailed announcements will be made on behalf of the government. Give these your closest attention. The government have made plans under which it will be possible to carry on work of the nation in the days of stress and strain that may be ahead …

Now may God bless you all. May He defend the right. For it is evil things that we shall be fighting against – brute force, bad faith, injustice, oppression and persecution – and against them I am certain that right will prevail.

For R.H. Lloyd-Jones, the outbreak of war seemed inevitable from the moment he heard the news of Germany's invasion of Poland:

> On the morning of Friday, 1st September, we were taken in as usual to Section HQ at Wilden for concentration. During the morning's training on searchlight duties I noticed at one point that all the sound locators, instead of being pointed up in the air as they should have been, were in a horizontal position and directed towards one of the huts on the site. There was a news bulletin being read on the radio, and our listeners were receiving, in this unauthorised way, the first news that Germany had invaded Poland, meaning in effect that war was now inevitable.
>
> As we left Wilden, to be driven back to our sites, cheerful shouts were exchanged between the occupants of the lorries, mostly to the effect that we would all see each other in Poland. One such shouted greeting has for some reason stuck in my memory; it was 'See you in Upper Silesia'. I don't think anyone nowadays would know or care where Upper Silesia was or is, but at that time it was a locality which was very much in the news.
>
> On Sunday morning, 3rd September, arrangements had been made for a civilian hairdresser to visit the sites. Sitting on a spotter's chair in the middle of the field while having my hair cut I heard a radio set which someone had turned on, from which could be heard the very pleasant voice of Neville Chamberlain giving the not very pleasant news that we were now at war with Germany.

Parents and children reacted quite differently, as Leslie Gardiner aged 12 remembered:

> Those words had hardly left Mr Chamberlain's lips when the sirens sounded and we expected German planes to appear immediately. My father ushered my mother, my brother, me, and the dog down the garden to the Anderson shelter at the bottom of the garden.
>
> As we hurried down the garden I looked over the fence to see our neighbour shepherding her two small children and carrying her small baby towards their shelter. What my brother and I found amusing was the fact that the two small children and their mother were wearing their gas masks and the baby was enveloped in a baby gas mask (a sort of large rubber envelope with a pump which had to be continuously pumped in order to keep the baby supplied with filtered air). Not so amusing for the harassed mother, but funny enough for a twelve, and a twenty-one year old.
>
> After a short time without any sign of the Luftwaffe, my brother decided to shovel some more earth on to the shelter which had been left, after its installation, with the light covering of soil which the workmen had given it. I offered to help big brother and we set to with a couple of garden spades. Apparently, inside the shelter, the sound of the stones rolling down the sides of the shelter sounded like gunfire and our mother urged us to re-enter the shelter at once. We did not do so, but redoubled our efforts with the spades so as to create the impression of a huge barrage. Our father then emerged from the shelter and upon discovering that we were teasing our mother threatened us with dire consequences if we did not desist. At that moment the all clear sounded and we had survived our first few hours of war.

The expectation of immediate air attacks also created tension in the RAF, as fighter pilot Alan Deere recalled:

> On the first Sunday of the war, a lone aircraft returning from patrol was plotted as hostile and a squadron scrambled to investigate. This squadron became split and sections from it were in turn plotted as hostile, and more aircraft sent to investigate until eventually the operations room tables, on which were plotted the raids, were cluttered with suspect plots. For about an hour, chaos reigned, and in this time nearly all the squadrons based to the east of London had been scrambled. I had trouble starting my aircraft and was late getting off and in the hour I was airborne spent the whole time trying to join up with my squadron which was receiving so many vectors [course instructions] that it was impossible to follow them. When I did eventually join up, the squadron was near Chatham where the anti-aircraft guns heralded our presence by some lusty salvoes, at which we hastily altered course despite the controller still insisting that we investigate the area. Not all the incidents … were amusing. 74 Squadron, led by 'Sailor' Malan, had also been sent off and their rear section of three encountered a pair of Hurricanes from nearby North Weald which, in mistake for the enemy and in the excitement of this glorious muddle, they attacked and shot down, killing one of the pilots.
>
> This truly amazing shambles – known to those pilots as the 'Battle of Barking Creek' – was just what was needed to iron out many snags in our control and reporting system and to convince those who were responsible that a great deal of controllers, plotters and radar operators, all of whom had been hastily drafted in on their first emergency call-up, was still required.

Betty Bullard, aged 21, had volunteered for the ATS (Auxiliary Territorial Service), and was working in a recruitment office in Norwich. She recorded the day war broke out in her diary:

Sunday 3rd September 1939
A terrible day. Great depressions but a firm belief to the last that it couldn't really happen. Sat waiting by the wireless. At last a fine speech by Mr Chamberlain announcing 'a state of war between this country and Germany'. Series of announcements. Black-out at night, cinemas closed, carry your gas mask, keep off roads at night etc etc.

It had come – decided to go to the sea with Geoffrey, Else and Margaret. Just arrived when M arrived for me to report at office at once. Went off in great excitement – all for nothing.

Monday 4th September 1939
Air raid warning 3am, returned to hall feeling a little nervous but went to sleep on the floor. I still can't think of Germany as enemy and feel very sorry for wretched young pilots. 'Raiders past' and went to bed. Office moved to Agricultural Hall. Major Tully in uniform – much more military. Spent day getting … ready. Norwich much as usual. Digging up cattlemarket and everyone carries gasmask.

Friday 22nd September 1939
[extract]
Went up to tea with Charlotte who is polishing up her German in case we lose the war!
I object to …
1) not being able to read in bed without having to grope about afterwards and open windows
2) being stared at in the street when walking about in uniform
3) getting no exercise (my own fault)
4) the noise the air raid warning makes. (A suggestion in

the paper that they should play 'Who's afraid of the big bad wolf?' instead.)

Mollie Wilson was a teenager living with her parents in Donaghmore in Tyrone, Northern Ireland:

> 2nd September 1939
> Mother and Daddy are so pessimistic we'll let Poland down, that they've given me the jitters. I feel just awful! Our house is in a good state of blackout. Worked all day painting blinds.
>
> 3rd September
> When Chamberlain made his declaration of war, there was violent thunder and lightning and rain shuttered down. I had always trusted rain too. No hostilities have begun but probably will have by tomorrow morning. All cinema shows and amusement have been prohibited as people are not to crowd together.

On the same day, in the log book for Warden's Post H85 at Paddington, London, the ARP warden on duty recorded: 'No first aid equipment, no formalin, no handbells' (these were to be used to signal 'all clear' to civilians when a gas attack had been dealt with).

Duff Cooper was at a meeting of the small parliamentary group of people who supported Winston Churchill at the home of one of their number, Ronald Tree (Conservative MP for Harborough):

> There at eleven o'clock we listened to the prime minister's broadcast statement that we were already at war with Germany. I recorded in my diary that 'we all thought he did it very well.' Our meeting broke up soon after he had finished as the house was meeting at noon. As we left the

> house we heard strange sounds and said, laughing, that it sounded like an air-raid warning, which indeed it proved to be. We walked on towards the House of Commons – Anthony, Derek Gullston and I. Derek said, 'We're walking pretty fast, aren't we?' which we were. When we arrived there we were directed to a room opposite the downstairs smoking-room, which was full of an odd mixture of people – servants, typists and the Speaker. We didn't stay there long but wandered out on the terrace, where we watched the balloons go up, which they did with great speed. It was a beautiful morning. The house met at twelve as arranged and the all clear signal went during prayers. I did not think the prime minister so good as he had been on the radio, nor did I think any of the speeches reached a very high level. Greenwood's was about the best.
>
> I took Terence O'Connor out to luncheon at Buck's. We both envied the people we saw there in uniform. They at least have something to do – and plenty to do. I have nothing.

Despite the warning which sounded in the south-east almost as soon as the declaration of war had been broadcast, the mass raids that everyone had feared would arrive almost immediately did not come. The Merchant Navy suffered huge losses as German U-boats and the Luftwaffe attacked ships carrying food and other vital supplies to Britain, but at home nothing happened and in the Phoney War, as it was called, people soon became bored by the Air Raid Precautions which punctuated daily life. ARP wardens who enforced the blackout and exhorted people to carry their gas masks were a source of considerable irritation and comment.

A letter published in *The Times* from H. De Pree of Beckley, on 21 September 1939, reflected a popular viewpoint. He argued that the ARP was 'an appalling waste of public money … excessive fear of gas bombardment in country districts [meant that] thousands of pounds have been wasted on useless equipment.' Much of the expensive and overstaffed organisation would, he said, never be used: 'Payment of £2 or £3 a week to men to stand about doing nothing is causing notable resentment among genuine workers in the country whose ordinary wages are under £2. Incidentally, the same feeling is caroused with regard to the excessive wages which are being paid by contractors to workmen on huts, &c., under construction for the government in many places.'

Anti-aircraft fire would be the best warning for those living in country districts and, 'based on this premise the whole of our ARP organization outside really important areas should be drastically cut down, especially as regards paid personnel'.

The wardens' log for Post 85 puts it more succinctly:

> 23rd September 1939
> 21.40hrs: Watch lights at 265 Lauderdale Avenue. Man most insulting.
>
> 24th September 1939
> Lauderdale Mansions, Lauderdale Avenue, light at back. Man showed most uncompromising attitude. Above reported to police … If light shows again, please ask for police to no. 64, and take him round to show him light.

Phillip Chignell recalled the horror of air raids which he and his wife had experienced in the First World War in Hessle, a town on the edge of Kingston upon Hull. He wrote to his sister about the impact of the declaration of war:

> Tuesday 5th September 1939
> My dear Ruth …
> … I am just going to tell you how it has affected us all at Hessle. My first remark is that it has broken up our little

family circle. All our four children have lived at home ever since they were born. You may not approve of this system but that is not the point. There are six of us, as you know, and we have all lived happily together until this time when Herr Hitler seems to have set Europe on fire with his terrible ambition. Of course we knew that something in the way of another war was brewing. It has not come upon us as a terrible surprise. The business seemed to have a definite beginning when Trigo came home from school on Wednesday with definite instructions about the school evacuation that had been arranged some time ago … On Thursday she went off to school with everything as arranged, temporary luggage, sufficient food to last. She came home at dinner time although we had not expected her and she then and there definitely refused to be evacuated, she just declined to go. We did not attempt any argument but we insisted that she return to the Boulevard school and tell them that she would not be evacuated. She went back and returned home for tea.

About 6.45 I went off to the bowling club and I left John having his tea in the usual manner. When I returned home at 8.00 to listen to the Promenade concert, John had gone. A dispatch rider had called for him and he had packed up and gone off at once. He left a form filled up to be posted to Smith and Nephew to say why he should be away from his work the next morning. We have not seen John since that day, but we now know that he is near Spurn Head with a gun battery …

… Of course you know that Katie and I lived in Hull all through the trying time, 1914–1918, when there were many air raids by Zeppelins. It is no new thing for me to hear gunfire or bombing in actual warfare and it is no new thing for me to experience the sickening sensation that comes to most of us when we know we are in the danger zone of aerial attack. I remember how father used to ridicule us for feeling like this and I sometimes wished that he had had at least one experience of an air raid. Nobody knows what it is like until they have had the experience. So Katie and I are not novices in this respect. We both feel we had our fair share 25 years ago and now we may have to bear the worry and trouble of it all over again.

At tea-time (on Friday 1st September) a dispatch rider called, this time it was for Henry. He packed up and was off in half an hour. Katie packed food for him and he went saying goodbye to us. We did not know when we should see him again or where he was going out … The vicar telephoned to me – on no account was I to have a light in the church or the vestry after 8pm. (re choir practice) …

… Harry returned home late last night – the authorities did not know how to sleep the 1,300 young men who had answered the call and most were sent home.

Ann Maxtone Graham's neighbours, Jane and Bob Badham and their son Michael (aged 13 when war was declared), met her at Southampton as she arrived back from the USA. Jane and Michael had gone to stay in Wargrave:

Jane said that she was wakened one night by Anna creeping into the room and whispering 'Jane, Jane, the sirens have gone.' They switched on the light, trying not to waken Michael. He, however, heard and said, 'what is it, a warning? Oh.' And he proceeded to read quite calmly while the other two quaked inwardly. Jane, in her excitement, filed her nails almost to the quick. At last she could not bear it any longer and went to turn up a tiny corner of the blackout curtain so that she could peer out and see what, if anything, was happening. To her complete surprise, it was broad daylight, and the gardener was bicycling up the drive with his gas mask on.

After two or three days, as things were quiet and there had been no raids, Bob had let them come back to London. There they had been ever since, living, as far as I could see, a perfectly normal life. And that's what I was going to do, go to no 45 as usual. Somehow it made everything seem so much easier to bear, to be going home, although I confess with shame, a little flat. It was like making your mind to jump off a high place and coming down about six inches. I had visions of myself dodging bombs and being homeless. Well, thank goodness, I had a home and, so far, no bombs.

When we got to London and started towards South Kensington, I nearly fell out of the taxi looking up at the lovely silver barrage balloons that floated high over the city. I had seen a few, but never so many as there were now. Hundreds of them, like little silver fish swimming in the evening sky. There were sandbags – sandbags everywhere, stacked against windows, built into tidy walls to protect doorways, and around police call boxes. In those days they were fresh and new, but as winter went on they rotted and burst, and at last a great many of them were taken away.

Home at last, and I felt as if the war was a dream. Number 45 Tregunter Road looked natural and just as it had always done when I'd come home to it before. At least it did until I opened the front door and found a funereal gloom. The blackout. I had forgotten it. Our hall and stairway had such odd windows that they couldn't be curtained. And the only thing to do was to cover them up with thick black cloth, firmly thumbtacked around the edges. We used to untack a small corner in the morning and pin it back, and then down it went again as soon as it grew dark. Oh, the thumbtack holes in my nice white paint! I felt I couldn't bear it at first, but after a few days one hole more or less didn't seem to matter. Once coming down the dark stairs I heard myself mutter, 'bloody old mole, that's what I am!'

… All this time my family in America kept writing and condoling with me on the horrible times I was living through. It was then that Judy [her youngest sister] wrote, 'I can't make any picture of how you live. Do you slink from cellar to cellar?' No matter what I wrote to them, they still persisted in thinking of me as a frightened, panic-stricken female, I'm afraid my letters to them were a little profane at this time, partly because I felt like a humbug having all this undeserved pity and worry poured out on me.

… Life was more or less normal. It was a queer time, knowing that there was a war but nothing dire seemed to be happening in England. I missed Pat and the boys more than I could say, and it was hard being alone.

But all those things I had got used to and I had Jane and Bob right around the corner. The nights I didn't go to them, they came to me. I made myself laugh, starting out to spend a pleasant evening, gas mask over my shoulder, knitting under my arm, flashlight in one hand and a cane in the other. I used to walk with this like a blind man to save the battery in my flashlight, as they were hard to come by at the moment.

… it was curious how the days flew. I suppose when you are busy they do fly. It seemed to me about five minutes from one blackout to another. It was odd how we got used to that, too, and couldn't quite remember what it was like to have lived in the days before the war when you didn't have to turn out the hall light before you opened the front door. How horrified and indignant we were if we saw a chink of light from a neighbour's house. The wardens and police were wonderful and spotted them almost at once. Sometimes they weren't very polite about it and roared, 'Put out that light!'

I couldn't blame them, for people were tiresome about it and acted as if they had been mortally insulted. Instead of being sorry and apologetic, they were rude and unpleasant when told there was a light showing. After all, they would have been the first to squeal if a bomb had come crashing down on their heads. But the warden said you couldn't make them realise it.

I was told that the British drove trucks or tanks over the moors to make it look like roads. Even flashed occasional light so that the Germans might think there were towns there. I believe they did and wasted a lot of bombs on empty spaces that might well have come down on houses and people.

R.H. Lloyd-Jones was posted as permanent staff instructor to 231 Searchlight Training Regiment soon after the war started. He travelled to camp at Blandford near Bournemouth:

> As we worked on the arrangements for receiving our first intake, as it was called, it was obvious that we were in for a busy time. There were well over a thousand men, due to arrive, all on the same day, all needing to be documented and fed and issued with their kit and allotted to living huts.
>
> We were in the Gym as the men came off the lorries that brought them from the station. There was much paperwork involved and many of the Intake seemed to be under strain. They had to be asked details of their families; some could not remember their children's names, one or two could not even remember their own names. I saw one recruit weeping and being patted on the shoulder by Capt. St Barbe in an attempt to cheer him up. Thank goodness we never had this emotional atmosphere again with any other Intake. As the war continued, it seemed men became less sensitive to the shock of being called up.

Attacks on shipping in the north Atlantic and in the coastal waters around Britain continued to take a heavy toll as Germany tried to prevent supplies reaching the country.

J.L. Stevens was 13 in 1939 and saw at close hand the battles fought over the English Channel and the North Sea, and the efforts to counter the naval mines laid by U-boats and the Luftwaffe:

> I had had rheumatic fever when I was 11 years old and had mitral stenosis so I no longer attended school. In April 1940, I was sent to a convalescent home situated on the cliffs at Broadstairs, Kent. We were allowed to write home once a week.
>
> I had been very interested in the planes which swooped low over the sea as they had large rings fitted and I had seen nothing like this. I was very keen on drawing so in one of my letters to my parents I drew a picture of such a plane. I did not know that all our letters were censored by the matron – really to erase our adverse comments regarding the home – but my drawing was blacked out. Later, of course, I found that the rings [were to set off] magnetic mines.

The first civilian war-related deaths recorded in Britain were as a result not of an air raid, but of a lone Heinkel bomber which crashed in May 1940 while laying mines off the coast of Clacton-on-Sea in Essex.

Mr and Mrs W. Gill of Victoria Road, Clacton-on-Sea, were killed, along with the four-man crew of the bomber. All that remained of the Gills' house was a mound of bricks; their son was one of the thirty-four who were seriously injured among a total of 156 people that were wounded.

The War Illustrated was published during the First World War and, as a weekly, in the Second World War until spring 1947. Its report of the Clacton crash, published on 17 May 1940, drew entirely on eyewitness accounts:

Mrs E.F. Thomas saw the plane crash:

> The plane was on fire. Several Very lights [signal flares] were thrown out of it and the pilot was apparently trying to find some place to land. Fifty yards up Victoria Road the plane hit the road, bounced through the side of a house and then went clean through to other houses, smashing them to pieces. A few minutes later there was an explosion …
>
> … Miss Joyce Redding, of Russell Road, said: 'One extraordinary thing was that, although every window was shattered and blackout materials were torn down, the electricity was not cut off and the district was a blaze of light. When half an hour afterwards an unknown plane flew overhead wardens hurried around shouting "lights out, lights out".'

Kenneth Harper, aged 17, a friend of William Gill, added:

> 'I saw the plane, which had been careering round the district for about half an hour, hit a house. One wing of it was left in the garden of that house, and it went over the Gills' house, knocking down a tree and coming to a standstill.
>
> I ran up to within about thirty-five yards of it when I heard a terrific explosion. The next thing I knew was debris flying all about me, and I put my arms around my head and ran. I had a very narrow escape. Bricks were flying all around.
>
> Bill Gill apparently got his father into the garden and went back for his mother, but the house collapsed before he could get her out. I suppose he found his mother was trapped and then he ran to get other help. Then, while he was out, the house collapsed entirely. When he reached us young Gill was without his shoes and his shirt was just about blown off him.'
>
> Brig-Gen W.M. Fordham, deputy chief ARP warden of Clacton, who lives in the road in which the bomber crashed, said he and his neighbours rushed to the scene. 'There was no

panic,' he said. 'The injured people were quickly attended to and taken to hospital. The ARP personnel showed that they have been well-trained. They were quick, and yet as cool and efficient as if they were on one of our usual exercises.'

Gen. Fordham added that the fire brigade and the AFS also did remarkably well. 'This terrible crash,' he said, 'has provided the biggest test to which any town's ARP service could expect to be put. I am proud of the way our fellows stood up to it.'

The *Irish Times* gave a more critical view of the event:

> [The fact that the] plane was circling overhead for so long before it finally fell was responsible both for some extraordinarily fine work by the town's ARP personnel and for a large number of injuries which might have been avoided.
>
> Many people were in the streets or looking out of windows when the crash came, and were cut by flying fragments of glass or pieces of bricks and tiles.
>
> As a chief air raid warden said: 'One lesson to be learned from the explosion is that people who had taken cover were uninjured, and an air raid shelter within a few yards of the crater in which the wreckage of the bomber lay was completely undamaged.'
>
> Some residents were inclined to criticise the authorities for not giving an air raid warning. 'I think,' said one of them, 'that most of the people who were injured were hurt because either they were looking out of their windows, having heard the plane overhead for so long, or were sleeping in upper rooms and had tiles fall in on them. Had they been in lower rooms or in a shelter the majority might not have been hurt at all.'

Members of ARP in a report centre. Reports came in by telephone or from bicycle messengers detailing incidents; locations of ambulances, fire services, first-aid parties, and rescue and repair services; buildings damaged and where casualties might be found; where roads were blocked and where water mains were damaged. The chart on the wall displayed this essential information and services were organised from the centre. *Courtesy of Kent Messenger*

3

RAIDERS OVERHEAD AND CONTINUING PREPARATIONS

The Phoney War came to an end in the spring of 1940, as German forces launched their Blitzkrieg ('lightning war') against western Europe.

Chamberlain resigned on 10 May 1940 after the disastrous Norway campaign had failed to halt the German conquest of that country, and was replaced by Winston Churchill. At the end of May British and Allied troops were hastily rescued from the beaches of Dunkirk, leaving most of their equipment behind. By the end of June, most of western Europe had capitulated – only Britain fought on against Hitler. The Luftwaffe bombed British airfields and ports, and attacked Merchant Navy and Royal Navy ships. It also targeted coastal ports and the Chain Home stations, where the newly developed radar was essential in giving Britain's anti-aircraft defences and RAF fighters warning of the approaching bombers.

The Battle of Britain began in July 1940. From then until September, the Luftwaffe attacked the airfields of RAF Fighter Command as the prelude to invasion. Any plan to invade Britain depended on defeating the Royal Navy, which could only be done by taking command of the air. Hitler intended to do this by destroying the airfields of RAF Fighter Command.

The Luftwaffe also attacked centres of aircraft production in cities across Britain. There were some raids on London, Liverpool and Birmingham. German losses from daylight bombing were such that night-time raids became the norm. Anti-aircraft defences such as searchlights and anti-aircraft guns, as well as passive defence such as air-raid wardens, ambulance and fire services, were still under strength. Attempts to deploy fighter aircraft to attack the bombers at night had proved disastrous.

Henry Beckingham was too young to go on active service when war broke out, so he was moved to another company of the Royal Engineers when his company went to France as part of the British Expeditionary Force. His account shows how, even at this late stage, Britain was poorly prepared to deal with the onslaught that was to come:

> Early in May 1940 I was in the courtyard at Borwick Hall when the Sergeant Major came up to me and asked me if I would like to go on a course to Sheffield. He also hinted that if I went on the course it would give me the opportunity of being allowed a weekend leave to be with my family in Manchester.
>
> The following morning Lance Corporal Acton, Sapper Andrews and myself left Borwick and arrived in Sheffield. Little did we know then that we were to form one of the first bomb disposal parties in England.
>
> Our course did in fact only last one day at the end of which we were given a drawing which showed how to deal with an unexploded bomb (UXB). It was assumed that any UXB would be found on the surface. The drawing showed how to build a sandbagged wall to which was added further sandbags. A small crawl-way was to be left in the wall to enable one to crawl in and place a charge on the bomb casing and thus detonate it in situ.
>
> We were then issued with a requisitioned old Austin car and told to carry out a thorough reconnaissance of the city so that in the event of an air attack, we could go directly to

any incident. Arrangements had also to be made to organise suitable store areas around the city where stocks of sandbags, corrugated sheeting, picks, and shovels could be kept.

We were attached to an RASC [Royal Army Service Corps] unit which was stationed at Endcliffe Hall, Sheffield, for pay and rations only. During the summer of 1940 we spent a pleasant time touring Sheffield and many afternoons playing table tennis in the YMCA [Young Men's Christian Association]; in short we languished in idle obscurity waiting for something to happen …

Our salvation came at the beginning of September when Lieut. Godsmark arrived in Sheffield with men of the 35th Bomb Disposal Section R.E. [Royal Engineers].

Some parts of the United Kingdom had no expectations of seeing the enemy at first hand. Pembroke in Wales had a rude awakening as Bill Richards, chief reporter of the *West Wales Guardian*, who lived and worked in Pembroke at the time, recalled later:

July 10th, 1940, will live for ever in Pembrokeshire's history for it was on that day that the county took the first shock of an enemy air attack. The air raid itself, carried out by a solitary plane, was a fairly minor affair compared with what was to come, but will probably be remembered as much as any, simply because it was the first. At precisely 10.12 a.m. without any warning, the town was rocked by a terrific explosion. There had been no siren and in those days an air raid without warning was unthinkable (how we were to learn!). All the many shops and offices workers looked at each other a trifle pale, and murmured 'Bombs.' Nothing happened. The sound of not even one could be heard. Perhaps it wasn't a bomb after all … Then, at 10.20, all speculation was ended by the sounding of the siren in the R.A.Y. Station. It was an air raid all right. A few minutes later the raider came in again across the town. There it was for all to see, a big, black Junkers 88, flying from east to west, high and close to the heavy blanket of cloud. I had ventured, albeit with extreme caution, from the 'Guardian' Office as far as the Bird in Hand in Lewis Street, and from the pavement there watched the plane in company with the genial landlord, Ald. Joe Gibby … As we watched, two black specks appeared beneath the plane. 'Birds,' said I, with more hope than conviction. 'Birds be d--d,' exclaimed Ald. Gibby, a veteran of 1914–18, 'They're bombs, come on in.' The explosions did not seem quite so terrifying from a crouching position beside the bar! Two stiff whiskies a few moments later (out of hours) did much to restore the equilibrium of both of us! During the next few minutes there were further explosions, between which machine-gun fire was heard coming from the Barrack Hill where some soldiers were 'having a go' at the intruder. At the time many people feared the streets were being machine-gunned. In all the excitement the sounding of the town siren – about twenty minutes late – went almost unnoticed. Some ten minutes later the Junkers flew away down south to return to its base, where, according to a later German news bulletin, the pilot reported 'a heavy raid on Pembroke where large fires were started.' Actually, the damage caused by this raider, in what must have been one of the easiest assignments any bomber crew could ever have had, was infinitesimal. The first bomb which so shook the town fell in the harbour between Neyland and Pembroke Dock … Had it fallen in the town it would doubtless have wreaked tremendous havoc … but miraculously no one was hit. The only casualties were scores of fish which, killed or stunned by the explosion, came to the surface and were washed ashore – to provide many a tasty meal for the people living in the Llanion area.

The other bombs, four or five in number and of smaller calibre, fell in and around Llanreath. This pilot was evidently after the oil tanks and although it was not generally known at the time, one bomb found its mark. But luck was with Pembroke Dock that day and the tank did not blow up. The bomb must have been a dud! Evidence of the raider's marksmanship was provided by a neat hole in the top of one of the tanks. Delayed action bombs being little heard of in those days, many people climbed a ladder to examine the cavity – and, months later, shivered at the very thought of it! This air raid, the first of many, was the sole topic of conversation in Pembroke Dock that day and for several days afterwards. To the rest of the county it was a matter of great interest but to the Borough of Pembroke it was one of vital concern. Pembroke Dock became really A.R.P. conscious overnight and braced itself to meet a grim period ahead. The townspeople were taken aback by the air raid itself but there was far greater concern at the almost complete defencelessness of the area and the fact that the siren was so late giving warning. We were soon to learn by grim experience that anti-aircraft defences in Pembrokeshire were almost non-existent and that the system of warning was to take many months to become efficient. In fact, during those early days bombs-before-siren became the rule. By the time the siren became of any use the enemy was beginning to switch his attentions elsewhere.

Mary Baker was one of many children evacuated to Tonbridge in Kent:

The Battle of Britain began while I was there. The sight of planes being shot down and parachutes falling is as vivid today as it was then. One day there was a terrified young German airman under guard in the town. I admit I felt quite sorry for him as he looked so scared.

One consequence of the unexpected inactivity at the very start of the war was that many children who had been evacuated away from cities and other danger areas in the first few days of September 1939 had returned home by the time raids on such targets started. J. Grenville Atherton, then a 15-year-old schoolboy, recalled his return to Stretford, Greater Manchester:

> We returned to Stretford from Macclesfield on our first day back at school on Friday 19th April 1940. Mr Albert Dakin the headmaster happily welcomed us. To ensure our safety he explained that all ground floor corridors were being modified and strengthened to make adequately-sized air raid shelters for the whole school, and that furniture and equipment was ready for use. He gave us a half day holiday, we gave him a spontaneous cheer and he expected to see us at 9am the following Monday when lessons commenced more or less as they were in 1939 before the interruption of evacuation.
>
> During the weekend one of my father's friends on the council showed him a notice from the town hall personnel department inviting applications for the post of assistant air raid precautions officer at £400 per annum. It listed 16 ministers to whom the applicant would ultimately be responsible. My father thought it was a joke.

In his diary, he recorded the first air-raid warning in Stretford:

> Today 20th June full moon 12.02am
> Stretford had its first Wailing Winnie siren air alarm at 3.30am. I put on my new sports jacket over my pyjamas and white gym pumps. My mother, father and sister just sat in the darkness and we opened the curtains. Our eyes became accustomed to the dark and the moonlight highlighted the polish on the furniture. We heard voices in the road; ARP

wardens. We thought it was quiet. We were ready to dive under the heavy oak table if needs be (we had no shelter then) but it was not necessary. After half an hour Dad went back to bed. We sat and dozed until the 'raiders passed' siren sounded at 4.15am.

Planes had dropped bombs on north eastern England and south Wales.

The next day we had another air raid warning from 1.10am to 2.15am but no raiders put in an appearance.

The prospect of a German invasion meant that the normally quiet coastal town of Southwold in Suffolk was on the front line. Typically for such places, its beach was littered with barbed wire and hundreds of mines were laid along the shoreline. A hole was made in its pier and two 6-inch guns were installed in the front garden of a seafront villa near Gun Hill to defend the town against naval attacks. The invasion never came but Southwold was frequently attacked by low-flying aircraft that swept in from the North Sea below radar cover.

Tom King began work in July 1940 as an ARP telephonist in Southwold police station. He was aged 35 at this time and was married with two young daughters, Rita and Liz. He had had a leg amputated in his teens after gangrene had set into an injury he had received after being kicked by a horse. His wartime diary reflects the long periods of quiet punctuated by bursts of frenetic activity as raiders hit coastal towns and airfields:

July 14 1940
Weather fine, began duties at 10pm till 8am for one week. Had a red warning at 10pm, all clear eight minutes later, 2nd warning at 3.15am lasting for four minutes, at 5am a yellow warning. PC Riches on duty.

Tuesday July 16th
Weather heavy rain all night.
Very quiet, no warnings, played cards with PC Guilliatt to pass the time away. PC Riches on duty from midnight.

Monday July 22nd
… new warning colours came through today. Purple is for dousing light, this washes out green.
Lights for warning are now yellow, first warning; red for action; purple as above; white for all clear.

Thursday July 25th
Weather fine early morning, cloudy later in the day.
Five yellows during the night. Very quiet in the morning and afternoon only one yellow, time drags – shall have to find a hobby.

31st July
Took Rita round the harbour and the marshes in the morning. She is a good girl and enjoyed the walk. Was pretty busy up to midnight when I came on duty. Played cards with the Inspector, Jarvis and Miss Allen. Taking the whole night it was the most active we had had. I gave out eighteen calls before going home for breakfast. At 1.00 we had a red through, I was in charge and switched on the siren for the first time, we also had two purples. At 2.15pm three salvos of bombs were dropped about two miles off the town into the sea. Bombs were also dropped between Dunwich and Wickham Market.

8th August
One red during the night and another at 6am lasting until 6.50. On duty at 08.00 I heard an explosion at 08.28am, report said that a bullock had strayed on to the beach and stepped on a mine. It blew the bull to pieces.

The first bombs to hit Southwold were dropped on 20 August 1940:

> 20th August
> Weather – Dull cool day.
> Had three reds during the night and early morning. Had one red through in the morning, three German bombers dropped bombs at Pakenham and Oulton, one German plane was brought down for certain. Red through again at 13.45, lasting for 10 minutes.
>
> We had our first bombing of the town, first raid started at 15.50. Two bombs landed in the back gardens of council houses in Hotson road, no particular damage to property, only windows broken. The second raid started at 18.05, plane came in from the sea and started dropping bombs in the sea, one landed on the cliff, one in the back of the vicarage and Glan-y-don by Mr Fisher's, and one between Field Style road and Hotson road, finishing in the hard courts. All told we had nineteen HE bombs dropped and four incendiary bombs, these fell near the pier, one fell in the station yard, and one on the marshes.
>
> Damage done – vicarage roof and Glan-y-don red roof premises severely damaged. Mr Bolderstone's house received a direct hit, Mr and Mrs Bolderstone injured also Mrs Sage who was in the house at the time of the occurrence. Main services in action, demolition and road repair gang. The ambulance took the three casualties to hospital. Incendiary bombs fell in the surrounding district.

During the 1930s, Croydon was home to London's main civilian airport, which became an RAF fighter station when war broke out. On Thursday 15 August, German planes overshot the airfield which was their intended target. Most of their bombs fell on a local aircraft factory, a perfume factory and a nearby housing estate. The sirens sounded seventeen minutes after the first bombs fell. Sixty-two people were killed, thirty-seven seriously, and 137 less seriously injured. Cecil Beaton, well known in the 1930s as a fashion and society photographer, was appointed an official war photographer and was an air-raid warden at the outbreak of war. In his diary he recorded his visit to view the aftermath:

> Went to Croydon to see real air raid damage. It is pathetic! The sirens didn't go off and 300 women and girls [this is an overestimate] were killed in factories there. The relics are poignant: a picture of the King and royal family among the cardboard containers that lie by the thousand among the white cocaine-like debris! A residential quarter also suffered, and one dwelling – luckily deserted – was completely demolished, its art nouveau decorations scattered far and wide. If you go there you'll find an unexploded bomb maybe a dud – maybe a delayed action. Better keep this side of the fence: Along one road, where a stick of bombs dropped, they've made a guy of Hitler, railed off a section and collected scrap iron, twelve and a half tons of it! In Germany everything is done by order. Here much is left to personal spontaneous effort. The funeral processions pass down the highway; everyone is calm and quiet. But one street beyond, life goes on as if nothing had happened, as if nothing could happen from one particular day to another – unless of course our number is called and, if it is, we are not likely to know it, luckily.

Across Britain many women, including Jim Purdey's mother, volunteered for ARP duty. Jim remembered:

> Early in 1940 proper brick built ARP wardens posts were provided. These were about twenty-five feet by ten feet, with

a flat reinforced roof and a door in the end elevation which was protected by a blast wall. There were no windows. Each post could hold about twelve people, and that was about the average number of wardens to each post.

Early in the war the name ARP was changed to Civil Defence and the Chief Warden for Croydon was a man named Captain Smith. Croydon was divided into districts and South Norwood became 'H' district, under the control of a District Warden whose name was Mr Luther. There were about six sectors in South Norwood, I can only remember H33 near to Goat House bridge, H39 in Regina Road, H45 in Manor Road, H50 headquarters in Harrington Road, and another one in Dingwall Road. Each post was under the control of a post Warden who had his three full timers and as many part timers as he could get. Thinking back on it today, I cannot remember any lady being in a senior position, although there were possibly more lady wardens than men. It was simply a sign of the times.

In late 1940 I became a warden myself. We were taught simple first aid, how to recognise poison gas, deal with incendiary bombs and report incidents on our sector. We learned that each poison gas has its own distinctive smell and exposed itself to anti-gas paint. The tops of pillar boxes and squares of wood fixed at a sloping angle were painted with anti gas paint, so that droplets of liquid gas changed colour as they dribbled downwards. If we saw this we then had to raise the alarm by using wooden rattles, similar to rattles used at football matches. Thankfully this drill was never carried out.

Incendiary bombs were another hazard. They were about 18 inches long and 6 inches in diameter, they burst on impact and showered the area with magnesium fire. They were dealt with by using a stirrup pump, or a bucket of sand or soil. One aircraft could carry a large load of incendiaries and cause fires over a wide area. In Croydon all roof attics were inspected and cleared of all combustible materials. The situation regarding incendiaries became so serious that people had to take turns at firewatching at their place of employment. This meant they had to stay at their workplace all night ready to tackle any incendiaries. A stirrup pump was a hand operated pump that delivered a jet or spray of water. It took three persons to operate, one to pump, one to direct the jet or spray and one to replenish the water in the bucket. If the bomb was in an open area a bucket of soil on it usually did the trick.

Bombs that failed to explode were another hazard. They could be defective or they could be one with a delayed fuse. These could explode unexpectedly up to three or four days later, and all had to be investigated by the bomb disposal people, by digging them out and taking them away and exploding them safely. This was a very dangerous occupation.

When a bomb exploded it caused utter devastation at the point of impact, and damage occurred over a wide area. At the edge of the radius of damage there usually were two sorts of damage. The first you noticed was that most of the windows were missing, usually blown inwards. One trick that everyone did was to criss-cross their windows with strips of sticky brown tape. This allowed the entire pane of glass to come in, in one piece, it prevented the glass from shattering, and prevented many injuries from shards of sharp glass flying everywhere. The window opening was then sealed with squares of what today we call plastic sheeting, which was fixed with battens. Although you could not see through this material, it did let the light in and kept the weather out.

Another noticeable damage was that the blast caused roof tiles to shuffle up the roof about six inches, thus causing the roof to become unwatertight. Slate roofs were not so bad, but with tiles, they had to be pulled down back into position one at a time, with the use of a flat trowel, a very time-consuming task.

Even a small bomb caused damage to water, electricity, gas and sewerage services, some of which took a long time to become noticeable.

In July 1940, Mollie Wilson joined the WAAF and travelled from her home in Northern Ireland to West Drayton in Middlesex. The diary in which she had recorded her and her parents' reactions to the outbreak of war was confiscated on her arrival in England by customs officers. She wrote regularly to her parents about her life in the WAAF. In mid-August she wrote about her experience of her first air raid:

WAAF training depot
West Drayton
12th August 1940
Dearest Mother and Daddy
I was coming to supper (yesterday) when I heard the wailing siren, followed by our own whistles (we pay no attention to outside warnings) and boy! Did I run or did I run! I wasn't scared, but in our own room we had been told to arrange a fire picket, and we forgot. So I rushed up the stairs and carried down a pail of sand, a fire extinguisher and a bucket of water to put outside the block. Some other girls carried down the other three buckets. Then I grabbed my mac, my gas clothing and mask, and ran. I slipped on the stairs and fell six steps but only bruised myself a bit. We all got into our trenches all right and sat for about ten minutes till the all clear came. The Germans must have been a long way off for we didn't see anything of them at all. It was jolly nice of Hitler to let us have the warning in the daytime and we were still in time for our concert …

... when I got as far as this we had another warning, 12.30. We stayed in the trenches until 1.20 but nothing happened again. I was a bit cross, 'cause I was terribly hungry but for dessert we had banana and ice-cream so it was worth it.

Vera Brittain, the author, feminist and pacifist, was a fire warden based in Kensington at the start of the war. A leading member of the Peace Pledge Union, she was in the *Sonderfahndungsliste* G.B. (Special Search List GB), the Nazis' 'black book' of names of 2,820 people who were to be rounded up by the SS following the invasion of Britain. Vera Brittain campaigned vigorously against saturation bombing. She wrote about the early days of the war and her experiences as a London fire warden in her book *England's Hour*, which was published in 1941:

The Post, like most wardens' posts in the metropolitan area, has been set up in a London County Council School. The other wardens on duty – a dental mechanic, a shopkeeper, and a paper-hanger respectively sit in a small office with a lofty ceiling. Three Daily Telegraph war maps hang from the yellow distempered walls. In a corner the Post's mascot, a thin and very lively black cat which walked in as a stray kitten six months ago, consumes his pungent evening meal of milk and fish. The Blue Cross label of the Royal Society for the Prevention of Cruelty to Animals, hung round his neck, entitles him to preferential treatment in a raid.

Pinned on the notice board are a medley of papers: lists of the wardens' duties and war stations, notices of lectures, a letter of appreciation from the Mayor and Chief Warden of Fulham expressing his satisfaction with the local civil defence work 'during the recent public air-raid warnings'. The latest list of air-raid casualties in the Metropolitan Police District shows that between Wednesday, August 8th and Thursday, August 9th, fifteen civilians were killed and nineteen injured.

We go out again into the area on a patrol of the public shelters. The Chief Post Warden accompanies us, wheeling his bicycle; in peace-time he is a glazier by profession, and was severely wounded in the War of 1914. Like his colleagues he wears an informal navy blue uniform, resembling a workman's dungarees. When the sirens go he mounts his bicycle and rides round the district, opening the locked shelters, and unlocking the First Aid apparatus and the shovels for dealing with incendiary bombs. If it is not locked up, this equipment provided by the locality for the public benefit is invariably stolen. The thieves are as difficult to detect as the slatterns who leave the shelters littered with newspapers or the greasy wrappings of their fish-and-chips.

These surface shelters, built of brick and roofed with concrete, are reported to withstand any catastrophe but a direct hit from a bomb. They are said to be impervious to bullets and splinters, and the blast from an explosion may rock but will not shatter them. Each thick squat building has an alternative exit filled in with sheet-iron or loose bricks which can easily be removed. A dim electric bulb provides illumination. If the raid destroys the local supply of electricity, a lamp padlocked to the ceiling will provide light from its separate battery. Before the London raids have become severe, these shelters are popular owing to the sound-proof material which shuts out the noise of anti-aircraft barrage and distant bombs. Later, when several direct hits have shown that they may become death-traps which increase the number of casualties, a widespread agitation for deep shelters will arise, and London's poorer population will invade the Tubes. Most of the surface shelters are built, or adapted, as annexes to public buildings; one adjoins a church and another a convent; a third is a public laundry reinforced with iron and concrete. The district is humble, with a mainly working-class population inhabiting small two-storey houses without basements or garden shelters. It is for householders who possess neither Anderson steel shelters nor basements, that communal brick buildings are now provided. Even when empty, their limited ventilation and their combined smell of concrete, new brick and Jeyes' Fluid makes them stuffy and close. When the public are in occupation, the atmosphere almost solidifies.

So far the residents of the small houses have taken to the shelters like foxes to their lairs. They have adopted them so effectively that they now camp there regularly with their blankets and pillows, rather than get up from a warm bed and emerge into the night when the siren goes.

'There's a whole set of social distinctions grown up in these shelters,' my friend the Warden tells me. 'The mutual exclusiveness of members at Yorkshire Luncheon Clubs is nothing to this. One group will refuse to enter the same shelter as another from their street. Then there are the quiet ones who won't share the shelter with children, and the Bright Young Things who play cards or darts and don't want elderly people. One old man regards a small communal shelter as his personal property; he sits there in his arm-chair and refuses to let anyone else come in.'

Just before midnight on a late August Saturday, in 1940 [she wrote] …

… We Londoners shall not be long in learning that this Saturday night was only a beginning. In the next fortnight, London has thirty raids, and her citizens visit department stores in thousands to purchase mattresses and camp-beds for their inadequate shelters. Gradually they become accustomed to nightly descents into the basement, and dawn trips back to their bedrooms after the sound of the 'All Clear'. We believe we are discovering how well we can manage with a few hours sleep or none … In the theatres

> and concert halls, impromptu performances now follow the programmes to fill the time during six and seven-hour raids. After a few days, most people continue their occupations when the siren sounds; often, writing my book or dictating letters, I become so oblivious of the raid that when the 'All Clear' goes, I imagine it to be another warning. In some of the big stores, 'roof-spotters' now relay a running commentary to the customers taking shelter below. 'There's a puff of smoke in the North-West! … Now there's nothing, so I'll put on a record.'
>
> … Already, if we are honest, we shall admit that we wake every morning with heads heavy and eyes dry from the interrupted night; that the daily sirens are beginning to challenge our powers of concentration with their insistent scream.

The Battle of Britain generally refers to the period 10 July to 31 October 1940. The first phase of the battle lasted from July to September 1940. In that time, 2,353 pilots from Great Britain and overseas flew with the Royal Air Force or Fleet Air Arm against the Luftwaffe. By the time it ended, 544 had lost their lives. The RAF proved harder to beat than Hermann Göring had anticipated. The climax of the battle came on 15 August 1940. Alan Deere was now at RAF Manston, a few miles inland from Ramsgate, the easternmost part of Kent. Airborne attacks over Kent continued throughout the war and already this south-eastern part of England was known as 'Hellfire Corner':

> For some time now, the Germans had been waiting for a day in which the weather would prove favourable enough to land a concentrated effort against our northern and southern fighter bases. It would thus be possible for them to determine to what extent our defences in the north had been stripped to supplement the hard pressed squadrons

in the south. August 15th was the chosen day … The first wave, consisting of about sixty Ju 87s escorted by an equal number of 109s and with Lympne as their target, was met by 54 Squadron as it crossed the coast between Dover and Dungeness. Against such odds, it was impossible to prevent the bombers reaching their target. Nevertheless we did manage to get among the Junkers 87s and to harass them throughout their attack, despite the presence of the 109s. It was an impressive sight … A mere handful of Spitfires altered the picture very little as, virtually lost in a maze of 109s, they strove to interfere …

… The first raid of the day had crossed the coast near Dover at 11.20am and the last enemy aircraft departed our shores at approximately 7.25pm, when a heavily mauled force of Me 110s, which had attacked Croydon airfield – an uncomfortable reminder to Londoners that the air battle was moving on to them – retreated to their lair in occupied territory.

In that short period of time I had been airborne on six occasions. Some idea of the intensity of operations can be gauged from the fact that a normal sortie averaged 40 minutes, and that on four occasions re-arming and refuelling was necessary.

So 15th August closed. The enemy had launched six major assaults – and many minor ones also in the south-east against airfields as far as Acklington in Northumberland to Middle Wallop in Hampshire. In all two thousand enemy aircraft had been hurled against our shores in successive waves only to be met by a determined defence which, although penetrated on occasions, never failed to close the gaps …

… Nightfall brought blessed relief to the weary pilots of the 11th Group squadrons who had once again borne the brunt of the attack. To me the reverse was true; I was shot down on the last sortie of the day and spent five agonising hours in the back of an RAF ambulance which bounced and bumped its way through the blacked-out highways and by-ways of Kent in search of Kenley airfield, only to finish up at the Queen Victoria Hospital, East Grinstead.

In 1940, 15-year-old Clifford Brownbill lived with his parents at Sheerness in Kent and worked at a local glass factory. His diary for 6 September refers to raids on oil storage tanks at Thames Haven and reflects the excitement many people – of all ages – commonly felt watching air battles between the RAF and the Luftwaffe.

6th September
Here is a commentary of a fierce fight.
The warning was given and a few minutes later Gerry arrived, the enemy planes were flying towards Chatham then our fighters tore across the sky and went for them hell for leather. I can hear our fighters zooming down and giving the enemy bursts of machine gun fire, they are coming back this way now, I can see them – there's machines everywhere. It looks as though the German formations have been split up.

I've got my eye on three machines. Oh! There go the machine guns again, a pilot of one of the planes has baled out while his plane careers off from the other two and disappears behind the clouds, smoke pouring from its tail. The parachute is dropping lower, it looks as if its going to land in the sea. I can see the pilot on the end. Hallo sounds like another formation coming over, yes there they are 12 of them travelling towards London. There's a huge column of smoke rising from the direction of Thames Haven, they must have set the oil tanks on fire again. It was on fire last night. I went up the hill and had a look at it through Dick's glasses; the flames were terrific lighting up the whole of Sheerness and Q'boro. This is the third time the tanks have

> been on fire in two days. Went up the hill, while up there the searchlights sprang up in the distance, a few minutes later off went the sirens, they were here again.

Both sides knew that as the autumn drew near, weather conditions in the Channel would make an invasion near-impossible. Even if the initial force crossed into England, it could not be supplied by sea. The Royal Navy and the RAF continued their battle in the air and on the sea, but the Luftwaffe's commanders now turned their attention to the concentrated bombing of civilians in the cities.

4

THE LONDON BLITZ

On 24 August, German aircraft dropped bombs on the city of London and to the east and the north. In retaliation, the RAF raided Berlin. In response to this, on 5 September, Hitler called for 'disruptive attacks on the population and air defences of major British cities, including London, by day and by night'. This first phase of the Blitz ran from 7 September to mid-November 1940.

The mass attacks on civilians that had been feared and expected for so long continued over London for fifty-seven consecutive nights. There were raids elsewhere too but the shift to targeting civilian populations provided some respite for the RAF which had faced heavy bombardments on its airfields.

In London, the bombing was concentrated on the city and the East End, the River Thames providing a shining silver path for the bombers to follow to the docks. This letter is from Will, an ARP warden in east London. Will was a schoolteacher in Leytonstone and wrote to his brother and sister-in-law in Abergavenny, Wales, about the first week of the Blitz on London:

> Leytonstone E 11
> Wed. Sept. 18th [1940]
> Dear Alb. & Bett,
> Now that I have a few minutes to spare I thought you might like to have a dispatch from one of England's many war fronts – London.

Somewhere in south-west London, after a raid, a fireman picks up a hose. A high explosive bomb has made a huge crater in the road. Gas, water and electricity supplies were often disrupted for weeks after raids and roads were blocked to most vehicles.

You know already that we've been getting it hot & strong up here ever since I've been back. Each night there is a raid warning lasting for 8 hours or more – mostly about 9 hrs, although last night it was 9 hrs 53 mins (from 8.07 pm – 6 am) with another warning at 7 am and three more since. Most days we get five or more warnings although only once or twice a day perhaps do we see an air battle. One is, in fact, going on above us now. We've had two long day-warnings lately – one last Friday from 8.55 am – 2 pm & one on Monday from 2.15 pm – 6 pm. School is a farce, as only half or less of the boys attend & we spend our time in the corridors which are our shelters. During these all night raids we actually get heavy gunfire & planes overhead for 8 or 9 hrs. Sometimes there's a lull for half hr. after the warning is given, before the show starts. Sometimes – most often, the guns and sirens go together. The last ½ hour before the 'all clear' is usually quiet.

I can't possibly tell you of the number of bombs which have fallen say within 1 mile or 1½ miles of this house – while Stratford, Bow, Plaistow etc are terribly smashed up. I told you, I think, of a bomb in Grove Green Rd. & one on a shelter in Forest Drive West. Later we had an aerial torpedo in Hainault Rd right at the end of our street. Bombs fell on a number of shops in Leytonstone High Rd & smashed 4 of them to mere rubble. Another bomb fell in the churchyard opposite Woolworths. Last Saturday night was the worst. An aerial torpedo landed directly on houses in Forest Drive West. Five were blown to pieces – not a stick of furniture even could be seen – only piles of earth, loose bricks & beams of timber. Eleven bodies have been recovered & they think there are still more to be found. Forty houses around (including the one whose shelter was hit the previous week) have been rendered uninhabitable & scores more in the street behind have had windows, doors, chimneys etc destroyed. Mr. B— lives 4 doors away & their house is badly damaged. The noise of that torpedo falling was terrifying – like a mighty rushing wind. I was lying awake in the bed & it seemed to be coming straight for us. The explosion made the whole house rock. 30 secs. later another aerial torpedo came and wiped out the United Dairies factory, a shop & two houses in Hainault Rd. That's the second aerial torpedo within 300 yds in Hainault Rd. A school has been hit & the workhouse in Union Rd. was struck by another aerial torpedo & several wards demolished. They are still digging for bodies.

These aerial torpedoes weigh about 1,800 lbs to 1 ton. The noise of gunfire, the whistle of shrapnel & the scream of falling bombs is appalling. Every few moments a plane or group of planes come nearer and nearer – the local guns blaze away & then a few bombs – sometimes near – sometimes further off. Sleep is impossible.

Last Monday I was put on duty as a warden for the first time since I've been back. My patrol is from the corner of Cavendish Drive down past our house to the bottom and up Scarborough Rd. I report when a warning comes. The post is about 150 yds down Cavendish Drive. Nothing had happened in our sector & I was told it was easy. The siren went on Monday at 10 minutes to eight in the evening. I reported at the post. The guns were already blazing away & planes were overhead. I walked back to the house – dodging into doorways when I heard shrapnel falling. I put on my mac & then it came – a 'Molotov basket' of 50 incendiary bombs on our street, a few on the flats behind us & a number on the railway embankment behind Mrs. S—'s. Some fell on Norlington School which is just across the line. I rushed out and blew my whistle to summon the wardens (3 of them) who were standing by. The whole street seemed ablaze with white magnesium glare. There were 10 fires between our house & the post. 94 escaped, but two fell three doors away.

I tackled one which was blazing under a front window and got it out quickly. Then the woman screamed out that one had fallen on a shed full of timber in her back garden & was blazing away. I rushed through the house & tackled the bomb with sand. Then I put out the blaze in the shed with buckets of water. The other wardens were working singly on other fires down their end of the street. Norlington School was blazing furiously & the Magnet Laundry next door. The Brigades were at work there.

The wardens of the next post were dealing with the fires in the flats. The remaining fires in Cavendish Drive we put out working together on stirrup pumps. One fire in an unoccupied house (No. 23) we did not notice for some time & it had got going. However we got them all out in really good time & with very little damage considering. The A.F.S. etc. were attending to the blazing school & Jerry was using it as a landmark & letting drop salvo after salvo of high explosive & the guns were blazing furiously. It was like hell let loose. I found several unexploded (or unignited to be exact – they don't explode) incendiary bombs which I had to carry away and bury in buckets of sand. Finally we mopped our begrimed faces & went to the post to write the report that all was in hand. Jerry was still pasting us. I came out on patrol again to make sure that none of the fires had restarted & 2 of the wardens came out with me. We had just left the post & there came the whistle of a bomb overhead – we dropped flat to the ground & it landed on the doorstep of 50 Cavendish Drive – only 25–30 yds from where we were lying. For a second or so I hardly realized I was alive. Then I ran to the house and plunged in to see if anyone was in there or hurt – it was like going into a fog with smoke and dust. Wreckage was all over the place. I searched the house and found only a dog shut up in the kitchenette & unhurt. Later we found that the people had gone to a public shelter for the first time that night. The front of that house and the neighbouring ones were smashed up & windows were broken over 100 yds away. When I saw the chunks of masonry & bits of iron railings that must have flown over our heads as we lay on the ground, I realized how lucky I was. Actually it was only a small bomb – a 25 or 50 lb one – Had it been larger, I might not have been writing this. To our amazement an 'all clear' went about 3 am but it was too good to be true. Jerry was back in an hour, pasting us again. He finally packed up just before 6 am. I had to look after the debris & watch there until daylight. When I got home I was more tired and worn out than I've ever been before. A neighbour brought me a cup of tea while I was on duty & Mrs. S—, kind soul, gave me breakfast when I came off duty about 7 am. There was another warning at 8 am & then I had to collect the unspent incendiary bombs and take them to A.R.P. Headquarters (I wish I kept a bomb now, as a souvenir). A phone message came through that a time-bomb was buried outside our school & that the area was evacuated. When I reached A.R.P. headquarters I was sent with another warden to examine certain places where it was thought time bombs had fallen. As a matter of fact we found none. It was 4 pm before I got a chance to sleep yesterday. It has been found out that the supposed time-bomb near our school was really a dud A.A. shell, so school is open today. I have rescued the fins of the first German incendiary bomb which I put out, as a souvenir. The bombs that fell on Monday night have done damage all over the place. Over 70 bombs – incendiaries and high explosives – are reported to have fallen in Leytonstone on that one night. Last night I was off duty – standing by in case of more incidents. I have put a mattress in the cupboard under the stairs & I lie there fully dressed with tin hat, torch, whistle etc. to hand. There was very heavy gunfire last night & I heard some bombs drop, but not very near. The Germans are dropping land-mines by parachute – one went off at the

Bell, Walthamstow & rendered 100 houses uninhabitable, and, wonderful to say, killed only 1 person.

I must confess that the long weary hours of waiting and listening through the night, quite alone in the house with not a soul to talk to, were very trying, but I am profoundly glad that Rube and the kiddies are away. This is no place for women and children. Many folk have packed up and left here recently, & I don't blame them. This dislocation of traffic has made it very difficult for business folk & often they have to walk long distances. This bombing has shown the disadvantages of trolley buses compared with buses. Once the trolley bus route has been hit, the route is blocked as trolley buses can't go round sideways. Nearly all the main line termini are closed & many suburban stations. However the biggest nuisance is the inability to shop, get a bath, haircut or go to church without being disturbed by the raids. We have had no gas for the last fortnight & are not likely to get any for the duration. You can't get any hot stuff in Lyons etc in Leytonstone – not even tea, & often there is no food as the motor deliveries are held up. Tea can be got at Baker's Arms because they are on a different gas system.

Well, that's enough about war. How are you getting on? I suppose you are settling in your new home & I hope you are very happy there. Are you having much raid trouble? Drop me a line when you get time – I know you are busy now. Give my love to Brian & Sheila. Boys up here no longer collect cigarette pictures – they collect shell fragments. There's plenty of it about the streets. If Brian would like a piece I'll send him some.

Now I must ring off, as I'm on duty tonight. It's 6 pm now – I've been writing this letter between whiles.

Look after yourselves.

Lots of love,

Will XXXXXXXXXXXXXXXXX

Letters were the main means of communication, even to people – generally the better off – who had their own telephone. Elizabeth Belsey was living at the family home in Keston, Kent, from where she wrote frequently to her husband, Lt John Belsey, who was serving with the Royal Artillery at Thames Ditton.

Fri Sept 6th 1940
Beloved
Here is your cheque-book and £ note – God knows when you will get them with the Post in the state it is. We got delayed and there were incendiary bombs here yesterday morning: afterwards the buses did not run beyond the Mark, and there were No Entry notices at the end of F Drive and Fishponds Road. Terrific explosion went off somewhere near in the evening. Crying scandal about the sirens last night: all-clear sounded at 5, when the sky was still swarming with German planes and searchlights. As soon as all was clear, the warning went again. I heard a lot of nasty bumps in the night and I sweated with terror and slept very little.

On the first day of the Blitz, Elizabeth heard the planes rumble overhead on their way to bomb London:

Sunday September 8th 1940
My darling
I hope for a letter from you tomorrow and will answer it, but meanwhile I send you a note to let you know we are all well, in spite of the ghastly blitz that London got last night.

We heard the planes at 8.30 (followed by the sirens), and then there was scarcely a moment's silence till the all-clear at 5. I had some nasty frights and did not sleep at all: we were shaken a bit but no harm done here.

John Belsey wrote the same day:

Sunday 8th September 1940
My darling Girl

I am now to be a member of the armed party who run around in a lorry during an air raid looking for (with intent to capture) accidental or deliberate Nazi parachutists, but this is a spare time job and not my vocation.

How are you bearing up in these appalling air raids? Please, my darling, do not get too frightened and do not get damaged, and guard my lovely Charlotte.

It was terrible last night. We were up for nine hours, and the sky was lit by the most lurid glow from the tremendous fires in London. I watched the flames and the planes and the guns and I thought of you and had a terrible feeling that you were in danger. Please, my darling, do not get hurt. Please keep alive for me to come back to you, to love you, and look after you, and see my beautiful baby again. I will keep myself safe for you.

I am now living without sleep and I suppose you are too my darling and that is much worse. As I do practically no work, it doesn't matter so much, but a peaceful night now seems too beautiful and remote to be considered …

Postal services were disrupted but letters were still getting through:

Wed Sept 11th 3.20pm
My darling boy
It was a delight to get your letter this morning at breakfast. I sent you a small parcel with a letter yesterday but I feel I must answer you with another. The sirens have just blown off for the second time today: let's hope as little happens now as this morning. Mother and Jeremy are out: I hope they will

find proper cover. On Monday night I was quite sleepless and terrified, with the result that last night, after feeding Charlotte, I fell into bed and slept like a log until 6, waking momentarily when the all-clear went at 4.45. I hope I shall be able to again tonight. I often think of you, my darling, out in a cold trench when I am warm in bed. Please try to sleep there, if it is humanly possible. I hope nothing too bad has occurred near you. We are all right: it's my belief that we are safer than we were – that they are now concentrating on Central London. We had four warnings yesterday, but heard nothing. It is dreadful to think of what is happening in London: the pictures in the papers make me feel sick. Sally says it is now quite difficult to get about London with any certainty. She will probably have to stay in London as the raids get earlier and earlier in starting. Jeremy has fixed a wire-netting frame in the landing window, to catch glass. He went to the Admiralty yesterday, and will probably do his advanced engineering course at Greenwich, but for the present is on leave.

You must not worry about me, sweetheart; I am quite well and feel much better than I did at first. I too had fears that you were in danger on Saturday night – but it seems we were both wrong! I will keep alive and well for you to come home to, and I will take care of my precious baby for you too. I would die for her if necessary, though it is unlikely that anything which killed me would not kill her too, as we are never far apart. You too must take care of yourself for me and her, as I do not know how I could endure your loss. I pray that all or none of us may survive this war; but not one or two …

… 8pm

Sally has just got home, exhausted. Holborn is the only station functioning between London and Bromley, and the crush is fearful. The sirens have not blown yet, but I expect them to any minute.

I am reading *Wuthering Heights* again and I find I enjoy it as much as ever before. This is strange for though I still think it one of the world's greatest novels, it is wild and formless and unrealistic. But perhaps that is why I enjoy it now – because it echoes my state of mind. It is a restless book and gives one no peace, even though it deals with life in a remote Yorkshire district a hundred and fifty years ago. Though it is unrealistic it is not unreal; while reading it, one lives in it – more so, I think, than in any other book I know. Through all its improbability, it convinces one of its truth.

On the whole, I think the nineteenth-century novel should make good wartime reading (damn sirens just going): its very size and ponderability make it somehow comforting. I will stop this letter now and send it to you in the morning. I had meant to catch tonight's post, but it had to be written at intervals and I couldn't manage it.

Take care of yourself, my darling …

The guns are banging and banging; but I pray you may have a passably good night.

With all my love
Elizabeth

The pre-war row over provision of shelters intensified. Those in poorer and cramped housing had no dining room in which to put a Morrison shelter, or garden for an Anderson. The government was reluctant to allow people into the tube stations in London but people took matters into their own hands – buying a platform ticket and staying the night became common practice. Phil Piratin, leader of Stepney Council, was a member of the Communist Party which had criticised the lack of provision in poorer parts of the country since before the war. He recalled in his memoir, published in 1948, direct action he led in the first week of the London Blitz to highlight the problems in the East End:

> Many people were without shelter, and every evening there was a trek from Stepney to central and west London to take shelter in one of the basement shelters of the large buildings there. The next morning thousands of bleary-eyed Londoners were to be seen on the buses and trains coming back to east London from the West End. The contrast between the shelter conditions for the rich and the poor called for exposure. This was done. When the blitz had continued for some days, we in Stepney took the initiative. One Saturday evening we gathered some seventy people, among them a large sprinkling of children, and we took them to the Savoy Hotel. We had heard from building workers of the well-constructed and luxurious shelter which had been built for their guests. We decided that what was good enough for the Savoy Hotel parasites was reasonably good enough for Stepney workers and their families. We had an idea that the hotel management would not see eye to eye with this proposition, so we organised the 'invasion' without their consent. In fact, there was some effort to stop us, but it was only a matter of seconds before we were downstairs, and the women and children came streaming in afterwards. While the management and their lackeys were filled with consternation, the visitors from east London looked round in amazement. 'Shelters,' they said, 'why we'd love to live in such places!' Structurally, the lower ground floor had been strengthened with steel girders and by other means. But the appearance of the place! There were three sections. In each section there were cubicles. Each section was decorated in a different colour, pink, blue and green. All the bedding, all the linen, was, of course, the same uniform colour. Armchairs and deck chairs were strewn around ... We had

earlier appointed our marshals to take care of all our people. They immediately made contact with the waiters, and asked for water and other such provisions. The waiters were most helpful. We were expecting trouble; we knew that the management was not going to allow us to sit there, just so easily. After a few minutes the police came. A plain-clothes officer said to me, 'What is it all about?' I explained. He said: 'We will have to get you out.' I said: 'O.K. – I'm curious to see what you do with the women and children.' (The blitz was on.) …

The management was in a dilemma. They urged the police to throw us out. We were able to impress on the manager that any such attempt would meet with some opposition, and that some of his guests in the dining room were likely to be disturbed. The manager left. He agreed to ignore us; that was what we wanted. Then we settled down. The first thing the marshals did was to call for refreshments. Many of our people had sandwiches with them and we therefore asked one of the waiters to provide tea and bread and butter. The waiter explained that they never served tea and bread and butter, and in any case the minimum price for anything was 2s. 6d. We said to the waiter: 'We will pay you 2d. a cup of tea and 2d. a portion of bread and butter, the usual prices in a Lyons' restaurant.' Three or four of the waiters went into a huddle, with one in particular doing the talking. He was evidently convincing the others. How they convinced the chef and management, I do not know, but within a few minutes, along came the trolleys and the silver trays laden with pots of tea and bread and butter. The waiters were having the time of their lives. They were obviously neglecting their duties, standing around, chuckling and playing with the children. The next day this news was flashed across the world. The contrast was made in bold headlines between the terrible conditions of the shelters in Stepney and the luxury

> conditions of the shelters of West London. As a result, the Home Office took special steps to improve the conditions.

Efforts to prevent large numbers of people from occupying tube stations were brushed aside by similar organised mass actions and by the sheer numbers of people going into stations in anticipation of the raids. Soon tube stations were home to thousands of Londoners. American journalist Quentin Reynolds recorded a typical scene at Camden Town tube station in his wartime publication *The Wounded Don't Cry*. American journalists such as Reynolds wrote regularly for the American newspapers of their experiences of the Blitz and greatly influenced public opinion in the USA.

> We climbed downstairs to the platform. The concrete stairs were crowded. You had to step over people.
>
> The platform was packed with people lying on the concrete. Some were playing cards.
>
> This is how thousands of families live at night in London – far under the ground. Usually the working man of the family arrives home about five-thirty. He'll find something hot in the stove being kept warm – if the gas main hasn't been destroyed. He'll find tea on the stove too. But his wife and children have long since left for the safety of the Tube. It is first come first served, and they went early.
>
> When Pop finishes his meal he joins them. They've saved a place for him. It may be cold down there and the air sticky with the feel of hundreds of people packed closely together – but it's safe. He and his family accept their lot philosophically. This is a new world and they adapt themselves to it.
>
> A man with an accordion came in and was greeted with friendly banter. He played *Tomorrow is a Lovely Day*, *There'll Always be an England*, and even the kids joined in the singing. Then he played the most popular song of the

day, *The Nightingale Sang in Berkeley Square*. Several 'incidents' have occurred in Berkeley Square during the past month and the accordion player commemorated them by singing his version of the song, calling it *A Screaming Bomb fell in Berkeley Square*.

They all laughed at that. All but me. I live in Berkeley Square.

It was getting late now. The Underground dwellers impose a nine o'clock curfew on themselves. The accordion player pillowed his head on the accordion. A heavy quiet settled over the reclining forms.

The guns and the bombs seemed far away. A train pulled in. Those who were asleep never woke, for noise is so much part of our existence in London these nights that it is only quiet that disturbs us because it seems unnatural.

Many people who had their own gardens did have an Anderson shelter. This was made from curved steel sheets bolted together and half buried in the ground. Earth was then piled on top. Andersons were 4ft 6in wide and 6ft high, and could accommodate between four and ten people, according to the number of panels used. But they were often damp and inclined to flooding. J.L. Stevens, returned home after her convalescence to Hornchurch, Essex, recalled:

In early October 1940, our shelter filled with water and we were unable to use it anymore.

One evening at the end of October we were sitting in the kitchen – I was reading, my mother was heating milk on the gas cooker. There was an air raid on but there was nowhere else for us to go so we just stayed there. We heard the sound of a German plane and guns were firing at it. My father decided to go into the garden to see where it was and then came in to say it had been hit and was coming down.

He went to the front door to check its progress and as it came down it jettisoned its load of bombs and incendiaries. Unfortunately, as my father opened the front door a huge bomb exploded in front of our house. We did not hear the bomb coming – I remember a roaring sound and everything went dark; a hole appeared in the side and rear walls of our kitchen; my mother screamed and shouted for help and cried 'won't anyone save us?' (She was constantly reminded of this for many years – my father thought it a huge joke.)

My father, who was in the hall, shouted that the kitchen door was stuck and he would have to knock it down – by that time, hot and cold water from the fractured tanks had started pouring through the ceiling. The front door and stairs had been completely blown away. We crawled through the hole into the garden and my father said we would have to go into next door's shelter. We had to negotiate round two incendiaries on the garden path – my mother in her shocked state stepped over them and consequently set on fire her nightdress and burned her legs. A huge sheet of flame from igniting gas came through the hole from which we had crawled.

My father went off to review the situation and eventually came back with a rescue team, as unknown to us the bomb had fractured the main water pipe in the road and this was cascading everywhere.

My mother, who had also been scalded by the hot milk, had to be carried from the shelter. I was dressed only in pyjamas and slippers and by this time walking was difficult against the flow of water; it had also started to rain to add to our misery.

The damage to surrounding properties was considerable and the crater extended over two pavements, the road and our front garden right up to the front door. The boulders strewn around seemed enormous. An ambulance was summoned to take my mother to Oldchurch Hospital, Romford; this duly arrived but broke down on the way and it was two hours before she eventually got to the hospital. She was, in due course, awarded a War Pension.

My father left me in the care of neighbours, not knowing where to go while he went to a first aid post to get a head wound dressed. Later he found me in the public shelter near Elm Park station – I was very wet and bedraggled so he borrowed a blanket into which I wrapped myself and he dried my clothing over a paraffin stove.

In the morning we went to a church in North Street, Hornchurch, which was being used as a reception centre for homeless families. I was given a pair of trousers, a coat (very thin), jumper, shoes and socks.

My father was given £10 as an immediate clothing allowance and, I believe, £20 for furniture. As we had no home it hardly mattered. After five days we had to leave and my father arranged that we should stay with his two sisters who also lived in Hornchurch. (We slept on the floor for two months.)

We had been very worried about our canary who had been buried under the kitchen debris but he was eventually rescued by the demolition squad some three days later. Fortunately he had sufficient food and water and had sung all day so his exact location was known. The larder door had fallen over his cage and this had sheltered him from the elements and debris which were constantly falling down. He was taken to the home of a PDSA inspector and a week later my father and I went to collect him. On the way a German plane suddenly flew low along the road and started machine-gunning: my father pulled me to the side of the wall of a house for protection. Having only just been bombed this was a somewhat unnerving experience.

Each raid left unexploded bombs – some delayed action, some simply malfunctioning – across the cities. Now based in London, Henry Beckingham's life of enforced leisure was over:

> We were now in the thick of the action – air raids every night and many during daylight hours. There was not time for leisure; we worked seven days a week from morning till late at night, and the only piece of equipment we had was a two pin discharger ... This company alone dealt with 470 UXBs during the last 14 days in September, therefore it can safely be assumed that they handled some 700 incidents in the month of September. Quite a staggering figure when one considers this company was responsible for the North of the Thames. No 23 BD Coy RE was carrying out a similar role south of the river from their headquarters in Balham.
>
> It shows the ferocity of the air raids when, in spite of the number dealt with in September, No 5 BD Coy had still 632 incidents on their books on 1st October.

His initial one-day training was supplemented by on-the-job experience. As he soon learned, most bombs did not sit conveniently on the surface.

> One incident I will recall which will show the luck, or fate or whatever you will call it, which followed me around.
>
> Having spent a number of days excavating for a UXB in the rear garden of a semi-detached house in Seven Kings' Road in Ilford, we eventually recovered the tail fins and knew the bomb to be a 250kg. This spurred us on to more frantic digging because we knew the bomb could not be very far away. At last we reached the filler cap of the bomb which needed more digging to uncover the fuse or fuses. Luck was not with us; the bomb had come to rest at an acute angle and the fusepocket or pockets were underneath.

It was decided to call it a day and to go back the following morning. You can imagine our sense of shock and horror when we arrived back the next day to find four houses all very badly damaged. The local residents informed us that the bomb had exploded one hour after we had left the scene. That was the fate or luck that repeated itself on other occasions.

One assumes that in all these incidents a clockwork delay fuse had been restarted due to the disturbance of the bomb. It was common for these fuses to stop with very little time left to run before they detonated. Thank heavens the ARP personnel always evacuated the area around an incident which kept fatalities to an absolute minimum.

On another occasion we were excavating for a bomb in the centre of Ilford when out of the blue a German plane swooped down upon us machine guns blazing as he roared past. I was in the excavation and the rest of our squad had taken shelter in nearby shop doorways. At this precise moment the floor of the excavation caved in, and that's all I can recall until much later when I regained consciousness and I was lying in a hospital bed in Ilford, with the worst headache I could ever recall. I again had been extremely lucky. During the raid a policeman and members of the BD (bomb disposal) squad who had been taking cover in the nearby shop doorways saw my head suddenly disappear; they dashed across the road and managed to get me out. I was unconscious having inhaled a good lungful of carbon monoxide gas, but luckily after a few days in hospital I was back in the unit and uncovering more UXBs.

The reason for the above incident was that a 50kg bomb had penetrated the earth before exploding. The force of the explosion had not been sufficient to break the surface of the roadway and thus form a crater, instead the explosion had created a sealed chamber, commonly known as a

'Camouflet'. Subsequently orders were issued to the effect that anyone working on the excavation had to have a lifeline around his waist which was secured to a picket at ground level. This restriction on movement resulted in this order being generally ignored, unless there was an officer around.

Cecil Beaton regularly toured central London photographing the aftermath of raids for the Ministry of Information; he recorded people's reactions in his diary:

> At the Natural History Museum the curator showed me the wreckage. The Times, he complained, had minimized the damage. Why, the herborium had been burnt out by an incendiary bomb! And that was the centre of interest of all the botanists of the world! Vitrines by the acre were smashed to smithereens, the carcasses of pre-historic animals had gone to dust – and the force of an explosion had caused a sheet of writing paper to cut a crack right through a mahogany cupboard door …
>
> … I went to Albemarle Street to see if the wax head I had seen among the debris of a former hairdressing establishment was still there. As I arrived a demolition squad was pulling down a large top-heavy facade. Whrump! The cloud of black dust eventually settled. I clambered over the rubble to find a new wax head lying, bald but smiling, among the cracked mirrors, glass fragments and wreckage of the ladies' beauty shop. The men working on the job were helpful, and when I asked one if he had seen lately the head with golden hair flying wild, he said he thought it could be unearthed. It was. The ghoulish head was produced from a mound of rubbish, and I proceeded to photograph it against the dreadful surroundings.

Suddenly the usual officious passer-by appeared. A little man with ferret eyes and a pointed red nose. I must show my papers. Yes, there was nothing wrong with the papers, but it didn't say you could photograph those wax heads – it wasn't right – the Ministry of Information would not want to show anything like that. I explained that, in any case, my photographs had to be submitted to the censor. But the discontent had started and now gathered momentum. The newspaper seller, who before had been so blithe and friendly, became truculent and grumbled that he wouldn't let me leave the spot until a policeman appeared and proved that everything was in order. A plain-clothes man edged his way through the gathering crowd, and whispered that everything was straightforward but that the feelings of the people must be pacified.

It was some time before the constable appeared and I was escorted to the nearest police station. After a few telephone calls everything was put right, but the constable explained that I had done wrong in provoking the antagonism of the crowd and a record should be made of the case. This seemed a somewhat empty formality since all the records had been destroyed by last night's bomb.

The raids soon became absorbed into the routine of daily life, as Clifford Brownbill's diary records:

23rd September
Had just finished washing when the sirens sounded. Mum and dad were at the pictures but they came home just before six in time for the King's speech. While he was in the middle of his speech the all clear was sounded in London. We could hear it coming through on the wireless so I got myself ready to go out for I knew ours would not be long. The all

clear went just as the King finished speaking and overhead formations of British fighters roared as if in salute when the National Anthem was being played.

The disruption to mealtimes became a near-daily occurrence:

9th October
All I seem to be doing nowadays is eating my dinner in the shelter. It is worth bringing your dinner …

The alert is sounding while a German is overhead. They have been flying around for about fifteen minutes before the alert. It's the same old routine, a raider comes over, the searchlights try to pick him out while the guns blaze away at the sound of his engines. This raid is the longest of the war – 11 and a half hours.

If everyone stopped work to go to the shelters when raiders were spotted, production at factories would be seriously affected – a point not lost on the Luftwaffe. Often a single airplane would fly over, its purpose being to disrupt production and daily life as much as possible. To counteract this, raid spotters, usually factory staff, would be stationed on the roofs of factories and would sound the alarm if the raiders were clearly coming too close for safety. Muriel Simkin worked in a munitions factory in Dagenham, Essex.

We had to wait until the second alarm before we were allowed to go to the shelter. The first bell was a warning they were coming. The second was when they were overhead. They (the factory owners) did not want any time wasted. The planes might have gone straight past and the factory would have stopped for nothing …

Sometimes the Germans would drop their bombs before the second bell went. On one occasion a bomb hit the factory before we were given permission to go to the shelter. The paint department went up. I saw several people flying through the air and I just ran home. I was suffering from shock and was worried about whether my own house had been hit. I was suspended for six weeks without pay. They would have been saved if they had been allowed to go after the first alarm. It was a terrible job but we had no option. We all had to do war work. We were risking our lives in the same way as the soldiers were.

Major war industries, such as aircraft engine production, were based in Manchester, making it a prime target for the Luftwaffe. It was bombed throughout the war, from August 1940 until Christmas 1944, when V-1s aimed at the city fell instead on nearby Oldham. This picture shows firefighters during a raid on the night of 7 December 1940; the heaviest bombing raids occurred just over two weeks later, on the nights of 22 and 23 December. *Courtesy of the Imperial War Museum*

5

SECOND PHASE

In November 1940, London had a single night's respite when bad weather prevented bombers from coming over. During the second phase of the Blitz, which ran from November to February 1941, the Luftwaffe concentrated on industrial towns, cities and ports around the United Kingdom. Cities in which war industries were working at full strength were targets as important as the coastal towns had been when the invasion of Britain – now indefinitely postponed – had been Germany's priority.

Coventry had experienced several small raids during July and August 1940, but on 14 November hundreds of bombers working in waves dropped incendiaries, high explosive bombs and oil bombs through the night. Dr R.V. Jones, at that time in charge of British scientific intelligence, later said that a miscalculation meant the German navigational equipment was not jammed as it should have been. As a result, the first wave of bombers ('pathfinders') were able to drop their bombs and light accurately the way for subsequent waves to continue the attack.

Margaret Chifney was a member of the Women's Land Army. She spent one of her days off visiting Coventry and, in November 1940, decided to spend a second day's leave there:

> My second visit I made with the other land girls and some soldiers from a local unit to a dance in the YMCA. We went in an army lorry.

After about an hour the air raid warning went but no-one seemed to be worried; we were told they don't come this far, 'they' being German planes. The next few minutes had the man eating his words for tonight they had got this far and came in force and to stay.

I had not seen any bombing in London. My five brothers were in the forces and my sister was in an aircraft factory and my father was making blackout blinds and curtains. My father and sister told me of the bombing for they were the only two of the family left in London, and until tonight I had not realised what they had been going through.

The warden was trying to get us all out of the building which was well alight by now but when we got outside every building seemed to be on fire and in the distance the flames were lighting up the cathedral. I was petrified and couldn't move, a warden dragged me to the ground as the scream of another bomb came but he left me to run to a woman who was on fire, he rolled her on the ground to put out the flames and took her to a shelter. I looked around to see if I could see any of the girls I had come with but more bombs were falling and I needed somewhere to shelter. The moon was like a huge torchlight and the roads had ice on them, the trees were sparkling with the frost. I heard another screaming bomb and threw myself behind a hedge and a short wall and covered my ears against the bang. I don't know how long I stayed, it seemed like hours, there were so many buildings burning now the firemen were helping people rather than trying to put the fires out, it was impossible. I knew that if I didn't move soon I would die of cold, how I wished I had my old breeches and boots on instead of a dress and these silly shoes, how could I run in these?

I tried to get an idea which way the station was. I thought if I got there I may be able to get back to base, so I got up and started to walk and then run a little in the direction of the railway, when I looked up and in the bright moonlight I saw a parachute with what looked like a dustbin on it so I found another wall to hide behind. I lay there, covered my ears and waited but the explosion did not come so I had another try for the station. I went up the wrong road twice and found myself almost back in the town when I recognised a black building that I knew was on the way to the station.

After what seemed like hours I saw the railway bridge and I thought 'at last' and then for the second time that night I was dragged to the ground, this time by a fireman. He said something and pointed to the railway bridge and hanging there like a chandelier was the land mine, the parachute caught on the bridge.

I spent the rest of the night wet, cold and very frightened, in a lady's coal cellar under her house. There were several other occupants. One poor lady had completely lost her mind; she was screaming and trying to get out saying her son was in the city – it was unbelievable.

How I got back is still a mystery. I had a ride in a car, a tractor, and the last transport I remember was a horse and cart but the welcome I got when I did arrive helped me to recover. I was so happy to see they were all safe, they thought I had been trapped in the building. I just collapsed in a heap and cried myself to sleep.

When I see people in films or on television falling out of windows with their clothes on fire I wonder how many people like me remember that it really did happen. It will stay with me forever.

When I returned to Coventry two weeks later to go home on leave there was nothing I could recognise, even the cathedral had only half one spire left – it was heartbreaking. I am pleased that the new cathedral has included some of the ruins – this way no-one will ever forget so many heroes, police, wardens, firemen and most people who were not burnt themselves helped those who were burnt. It amazes me that anyone came out of there alive.

H.R. Clothier had started a new job as head of the Invoice Certification Department of Daimler Aero Engines as the war broke out and had moved to Coventry. Of the first raid he wrote:

The sirens went and all hell was let loose. The next day at work a colleague at work suggested Lilian [his wife] and I stay at his place at Narborough in Leicester. So Lilian and I got ready when I got home and got to the town square and waited for the Leicester bus. Then the sirens went and we were well down the queue. Was I frightened? I'd got nerves like steel – steel that's long since had metal fatigue. My heart was in my boots. I must say about Lilian – she kept calm. The night before, when we went down to the shelter, everyone was quaking and she just sat on the steps knitting. Now I look back, her steady calm must have calmed the other inmates. Anyway we slowly moved up the queue, amid the sound of droning aeroplanes and then I saw the bus was full. Oh dear! But he was a tolerant bus conductor and let us get on. God I was relieved when the bus drove away. Narborough was a haven – I really thanked my colleague – not a sound all night.

In late 1940, Claire Lowry applied to join the Women's Royal Naval Service (WRNS). She went to their Portsmouth offices the morning after another night's bombing:

People were streaming out of Portsmouth, with cases, bundles, prams and bicycles – all carrying as many belongings as they could muster. The reason was clear – the devastation was terrible – terraces of houses, pubs, shops, all in smoking ruins.

The people had no homes anymore, so they were on their way to the country, no doubt village halls, cottages, would take them in and the WVS would provide food and comfort as they always did in those times. Meanwhile, I had to pick my way through the rubble along Hampshire Terrace and the police stopped me, saying it was too dangerous to go further.

As my Grandmother was terrified of the air-raids, my Auntie and Uncle would stay with her overnight. There was an air raid shelter at the end of the road, so when the raid was on, they would rush to the shelter, whilst Uncle would rush to his bank to fire-watch. Grandmother could not walk very fast, so eventually they stayed in her house whenever a raid was on. One night they were in the back of the house when a bomb was dropped on a house nearby. Auntie thought that the roof had been blown off their house, so they tried to open the front door, but it was jammed, so they struggled in the dark to the front room to get out of the window, but Grandmother said, 'Look, the whole of the front is blown out', so they calmly walked out through the blown out window. Hurriedly, hustling grandmother along the avenue, Auntie went back to her flat in London Road, and they sat and recovered from the shock, until Uncle rejoined them. The next day, Auntie returned to the shattered house, to ascertain the damage. In the daylight, she saw that the whole front of Grandmother's house was devastated, but when Auntie carefully walked through the debris into the front room of the house, an amazing sight met her eyes. The glass blown from the large bay windows had splintered into hundreds of pieces, and they were firmly embedded into the walls of the room. In the sunlight the glass flashed like chandeliers, and tinkled like Chinese chimes.

The house was unliveable, so Grandmother, Uncle and Auntie went to Lovedean to live, until the repairs were made.

Incendiary bombs caused massive destruction and so, in 1941, the government created the Fire Guard. This expanded dramatically the volunteer Street Fire Parties and Firewatchers, and made fire-watching duties compulsory in towns and cities, beyond factories and other essential areas. This poster encouraged people to sign up for training to deal with incendiaries. *Courtesy of The National Archives*

Manchester was another city in which major war industries were based. The first attacks were fairly light, but over Christmas 1940 Manchester experienced a massive raid which J. Grenville Atherton recorded in his diary. His father was in charge of the works engineering department at Metropolitan Vickers which built Lancaster bombers and which he refers to as 'Metrovickers':

> Sunday 22nd December 1940
> 4th in Advent. Shortest Day:
> The 'raiders passed' went at 3.45 am. Got up at 8 am. Sirens went again 10.30am so went for ride round Flixton. Roads quiet. Tyre punctured in back wheel as I got home.
>
> Took liqueur glasses to Auntie Jessie for Christmas present. After tea called at Bernard's. At 6.40 pm sirens went followed by terrific gunfire. Went in their shelter with his two sisters and brother Ian.
>
> Stayed till 10.00 pm then went home.
>
> Fires burning over the dock area. Trafford Park factories on fire. All sky lit orange, red, pink. All quiet between guns. Dead silent … Always this stillness and silence. No 'in-between noises' unless a bomb lands near.
>
> Heard ambulance/fire bell in distance.
>
> Ran to Sevenways [a road junction] and went in the shelter; nobody in. A special constable poked his head in. Told me to stay. Ignored him because I knew my parents worried about me. Ran out. Just then more bombs landed on nearby industrial complex of T[rafford] Park; it sent along a cold breeze. Blast. Still not a soul in sight. Windows of houses reflect bright pink glow, pavements pink. Pink sunshine at night – eerie but interesting.
>
> Ran up driveway of first house and pinched their metal dustbin lid, held it over my head against raining shrapnel and scooted home to family. No neighbours in our shelter for a

change. Thankful to be home safe. All OK. Planes overhead continuously. Searchlight beams in field at back bounced off dirty low clouds and smoke. Bombs and gunfire all mixed up, can't tell which is which.

Commenting some years later and quoting further from his diary, he added:

We had been in the shelter since 10.30 last night (Sunday). The guns opened fire again and again, the noise was ear splitting. The 14-inch wall of our surface shelter, though reinforced with steel, shook many times. Mum looked pale and fretted about people being killed. She had dealt with hundreds of front line casualties having spent a short time in France in 1914 in the Voluntary Aid Detachment of the Red Cross and four years at Elm Bank war emergency hospital in Eccles until 1918, but she said this is a different war …

Dad looked serious. He seemed very calm outwardly, but uneasy. My sister was tired out and went to sleep. I, as usual, became restless and fidgety and wanted to go out to have a look. I felt better when I could see what was going on instead of letting my imagination run riot.

A fairly bright orange and greenish light of burning warehouses and chemicals blanketed the whole of the north. Stretford, Old Trafford and the densely populated streets of Hulme seemed to be receiving the worst of it, as was confirmed later. Fires could easily be seen flaring over the centre of Manchester, and occasional bright flashes showed up against the night sky as more flammable material took hold. Canisters of small magnesium incendiary bombs fell everywhere. They were nasty little things. All right for fireworks but not when they were aimed at your head. Later on they carried a small explosive charge to deter you from coming too close.

Outside most houses for emergency use were a bucket of sand or water, a stirrup pump and its 30ft of hosepipe. In addition we kept our bath full of cold water.

One o'clock, two o'clock, three o'clock, four, five and six o'clock, it went on. Our eyes smarted with the smoke accompanied by a strong smell of cordite [his diary continued] 'not unlike our school chemy lab. Near Cowburn's down the road in Trafford Park were open railway wagonloads of sulphur as used for woollen bleaching amongst other things. It was evil, poisonous stuff when it caught fire or just smouldered …

… 'Read "Everybody's," [a popular magazine] and nodded off. Heard shrapnel hit tiles and rattle into the gutters. This is definitely the worst raid we have had. Dozing and waking.

'Bomb hit electricity distribution kiosk round corner on Urmston Lane and put out elec. stove and lamp. Lit candles in jam jars.

'All clear at 6.16 am. It has been 11 hours 36 minutes.'

For good measure we had a short alarm at 6.45 am. You can imagine our mixed feelings – but all clear 45 mins later.

Our little pet budgie was dead, all windows in glass vestibule at the side of the house broken and garage doors blown off. Sticky tape on windows not much good.

Monday 23rd December 1940

Father went to work without any sleep. He was quite unflappable. I am quite sure having a routine job to get on with, even if it is just doing the housework, helps you to keep going.

He said what we all need is time. Time to go to work. Time to put up with the raids. Time to catch up on sleep.

His department was responsible for the entire running of the hundreds of acres of factory and goodness knew what damage he was going to find.

My sister and I went to bed for an hour or two then got up and swept away broken glass and plaster. It was everywhere, in the carpet, curtains, even stuck in the soap and needless to say I cut my finger. Having no electricity was a nuisance. I bought a new cycle tyre for 7/4d. (previously 6/1d.) plus purchase tax 1/3d. Eddie and I went for a short ride round the district. Saw lots of bomb craters. Many new houses badly damaged in Humphrey Park Estate a mile away. Half of one avenue destroyed – 11 houses missing. Some killed. My friend Eddie and I felt guilty and intrusive and rode away.

In Trafford Park dozens of warehouses and factories damaged and still smoking. Rosser's timber yard on fire. All that lovely wood still blazing. They must have drained the Bridgewater Canal and Manchester Ship Canal nearly dry, or so it seemed.

A flour miller's was on fire – thousands of tons of it. Firemen were covered in sticky dough from the hose water. We had a good laugh, not at them, but with them, though there were tears in their laughter due to exhaustion. Two firemen lay on the ground with burnt hands, their faces white with flour, eyes red rimmed, like crumpled clowns …

… Smoke and dust seemed to be blowing in the cold wind from all directions. Came home via MetroVickers which had been hit, but I could see my father's office window from Westinghouse Road and his office block looked unharmed. A water main had been torn up within the factory and firemen were pumping it away.

Luckily few people were injured because they had a spotting system to warn if raiders approached near, and because yesterday was a Sunday there were not as many as usual on the night shift and most of the offices were empty. There were about 1,000 firemen including auxiliaries, and several shelters to take many workers and staff, probably several thousand.

> The main 'tunnel' shelter underneath the main 'aisles' or machine shops would withstand anything but a direct hit. It had an operating theatre and full time medical staff and fifty beds for casualties …
>
> … Families went back to their houses to collect bedding and blankets and warm clothing. There was insufficient organisation for the salvaging and reclamation of clothes and property. If they could not find their own home they just took anything suitable that was lying about. Most houses were just a shell, with bricks and floorboards spilled out in a sloping heap on to the cobbled streets. There was no space for ambulances to drive. Also no room for Anderson shelters in many cases because there were no gardens, although some had put them in the back yard. Consequently more were killed and crushed and burned.

The bombers were back the following night, 23 December:

> Father came home from work tired out. He said that two landmines (parachute bombs) had caused fearfully expensive damage and he was in the process of setting up a programme of repair work which was the main task of his department, Works Engineering, and in addition carried the full responsibility for all ARP services throughout the massive plant.
>
> After tea we continued to tidy the house, carrying on as normal, when the sirens sounded their wavy 'up and down' howling. Fires were still alight in the darkness so no doubt Jerry easily found his direction …
>
> … My sister had spent the night with friends in Sale, not far away, and they came back with her in the morning to see if we were safe. Apart from the usual cracked plaster and most of the leaded-lights being broken, we were thankful for no injuries. Nearly every house in Melville Road was destroyed

by a land mine. There were several casualties. Albert's wife lost her arm. To save his life, firemen had to chop off a young lad's foot with an axe because he was trapped in a collapsing building. They both recovered. The girls' high school where my sister attended received a direct hit, a merciful blessing the girls were on holiday for Christmas. Uncle Fred's house in Ravenswood Road next to the school lost its roof. Uncle Tom's house was ripped open while they were sheltering. Metrovickers was hit again and the main turbine and generator workshops damaged badly.

The centre of Manchester was on fire, water mains broken, and offices and banks and warehouses adjacent to Mosley Street and Piccadilly were blazing fiercely. The commercial centre of the city came off worse than factories and mills in the northern suburbs. A large part of the historic Free Trade Hall, home of the Halle orchestra, was destroyed by fire.

Nearer home a small HE [high explosive] bomb went off in Mr Dakin's (our headmaster) front garden in Urmston Lane round the corner and in Arlington Road two houses only eight doors away got a direct hit.

After helping his mother nail weatherproof sheeting to the window frames, J. Grenville Atherton sets off to the safety of his aunt's house outside the city:

Main roads into Manchester were impassable due to debris and collapsed buildings, smouldering fires, telegraph poles uprooted, smashed furniture, vehicles and police barriers and bomb craters and so on. Burst water mains and sewage had formed deep puddles. Being Christmas Eve few services were available.

I got off the bus half a mile from the city centre, carrying my little 'evacuation' suitcase over concrete blocks, fallen walls and steel girders twisted with heat. Danger notices pointed out deep basements that were not easily recognised. The main shopping centres, Deansgate and Market Street, were smashed to bits, a chaotic litter. Buildings were knocked down and shops and offices open to the cold grey sky for everyone to see, still crumbling and cracking. Ladies and menswear, bedding, household goods, furniture, books, foodstuffs were scattered in confusion. Anybody could pick it up and probably did. The wind was just blowing it all to waste.

There must have been bodies under all that mess yet many were saved because the first night of the blitz was a Sunday when the town was relatively empty. There were others like me carrying some luggage out of the city. I called to a man, and he replied that Piccadilly bus station 'had gone' but that buses were going north from Fairfield Street. Otherwise it was strangely and unexpectedly quiet. No crowds of sightseers. No heavy demolition gangs. I saw firemen, wardens and police and rescue workers climbing in and out of the delicately balanced shells of buildings which looked as if they would crumble like a biscuit at a touch, looking and listening for any trapped victims.

Eventually he arrives at a hotel and meets his relatives.

Christmas Day
My father telephoned from work to wish us a happy Christmas under the circumstances. He and mother were all right. We ate a lovely Christmas dinner with 8 other guests present. Afterwards some of us went for a walk round the village. It was fine and cold with a blue sky. No air raids to worry us.

The parish church had a decorated tree next to the bell tower. That evening my aunt (the welfare officer) attended a special service to pray for the victims of air raids everywhere.

Boxing Day

Today we all transferred to the Hanging Gate Hotel across the moors on the Huddersfield road to a village called Diggle. The landlord, appropriately named Mr. Moorhouse, was a big, fat individual, bald, with a lady I thought was his mother but was his wife. He said he was willing to take in any evacuees and homeless people from Manchester as long as they could pay, and the blitz was good for business and laughed his head off at his 'joke'. He seemed quite unconcerned.

Outside the hotel, which was beautifully furnished and appointed, was a hand painted sign: 'This gate hangs well and hinders none. Refresh and pay, and carry on.' We could pay. But what if we could not?

... On Friday the newspapers were published, which said a north west town had been attacked. It was rather non-committal due to censorship until the Germans admitted they had bombed Manchester. It was stated in the paper that much needless suffering had been caused to survivors because some emergency services had been on holiday. This same day Auntie Mollie, and Barbara and Joan (they were a couple of years older than I) went by bus on a very cold day to Salford and Stretford town halls, respectively, to try to arrange urgent repairs to their home in Salford and Uncle Fred's in Stretford. They were told not to be impatient and that they were not the only ones with a problem and if they could afford to spend time at a hotel they were obviously not desperate for help. They had lost all their ration books and identity cards and insurance policies. They were so upset at the callous attitude they were in tears. Both uncles had served throughout the first world war and they managed to get some satisfaction the following week. My other aunt had a lingerie shop on Regent Road, Salford, which had its windows smashed and she had no problem at all with the

> town hall officials. All our homes were eventually repaired by local tradespeople after submitting claims to the assessors who came round to inspect the damage on behalf of the War Damage Commission. The money was either paid to you or to the contractor who carried out the repairs.

Experience showed the importance of spotting incendiary bombs quickly, before they caused major fires. As with many other areas of ARP, the initial response to the call for volunteers was patchy. The Fire Watchers Order, introduced in September 1940, compelled owners of businesses to ensure that someone on the premises was responsible for fire watching at all times.

Further legislation in October 1940 gave ARP wardens and others the power to enter premises to prevent fires from spreading. On 29 December 1940, incendiary bombs caused massive fires across the city of London.

Reginald Bell was Group Co-ordinating Officer of the London Civil Defence Region:

> On the night of 29th December the tide reached its lowest (an abnormally low) ebb ... The night was rainless and clear.
>
> It was in these conditions, exceptionally favourable to fires in the centre of London, that the Luftwaffe was sent forth upon a deliberate attempt to burn the city to the ground.
>
> At 6.30pm the attack began. Basket after basket of incendiaries clattered on the roofs and streets of the City of London. All round St Paul's Cathedral fires sprang up and spread. Fire bombs fell on the cathedral roof but by the devoted activity of watchers who knew every nook and cranny of the terrain all were cast off and the Cathedral was saved.
>
> Other firewatchers, with equal diligence and success, extinguished every incendiary bomb which fell on the Guildhall. Alas their efforts were in vain. Thousands of bombs on unattended or inaccessible roofs all round started

fires which roared like furnaces in the high wind. Embers and incandescent particles varying in size from half a crown to a saucer swirled into the air and swept like a sparkling snowstorm through the streets and among the chimney-tops, laying a blanket of glowing brands upon roofs and gables …

The control centre, overwhelmed by messages calling for pumps to attend fires and surrounded by circles of flames, took what essential records and equipment they could to a reserve location.

The water supply of London failed, important mains being shattered by High Explosive bombs … only by dragging heavy suction-pipes across the mud from the fireboats in mid-stream could water be brought to the bank. In the river-bed, hour by hour, firemen toiled in the eerie glare from a wall of fire, heaving, straining and coaxing slimy pipes and slippery couplings into a battery of lines for vital water supply.

… two officers and fourteen men were killed and 250 officers and men injured in fighting the fifteen hundred fires that blazed in London that night.

As the tide turned the fires were brought under control. The real damage had been done in the first five hours of the attack but daylight showed the extent of the damage:

Mountains of calcined stone lay in the streets; forests of twisted girders sprouted … from red-hot basements which glowed sullenly for days.

Millions of gallons of water poured uselessly away from fractured mains so deep under heaps of rubble that turncocks and water officers were faced with hopeless problems. In provision shops roast carcasses, fowls and foodstuffs filled the air with strange, mixed odours.

This raid quickly became known as the Second Great Fire of London. The damage caused by incendiaries was a particular cause for concern. On 31 December 1940, Herbert Morrison broadcast on the radio that 'Britain shall not burn' and shortly afterwards assumed powers to conscript people into a new group: the Fire Guard.

The new organisation took in the previous schemes of Firewatchers and Street Fire Parties and people were organised and trained locally by ARP services. The aim of the Fire Guard was to spot incendiaries, put them out or call the National Fire Service if the fire looked like it was getting out of control. Members of the Fire Guard were organised into stirrup pump teams, each comprising three people and working on rotas. In towns and cities the aim was to have seven stirrup pump teams to every thirty houses or 150 yards.

Rose Uttin, aged 41 when she started this diary, was a member of a fire party in Wembley, Middlesex. She lived with her husband Bill, mother, and daughter Dora, who was aged 13 when the war broke out. Bill was also a member of the fire party at home and in his workplace at the Royal Exchange in the city of London:

20th January 1941
11.30pm and no alert so we are off to bed. Still downstairs in the lounge of course – I wonder how long it will be before we can safely sleep upstairs again.

At 4am we were awakened by persistent knocking at the front door. I thought at first something had happened to mother but it was the firewatcher. He had made a mistake and he didn't know how to contact the next couple. He sounded so tired but said he could not go home until he found them – rather like Mary and her lamb; it has not stopped raining since 4 o'clock yesterday so expect the shelter is full of water. Something will have to be done about it – an added base of concrete Bill thinks.

22nd Jan

We had this evening at 7.30 am our second meeting and we gained 21 new 'watchers' – now it is hoped that it will mean one night on duty in 9 instead of the 6 as first planned. It is imperative we keep awake for the sirens are not penetrating enough when one is sound asleep. This war has made us meet our neighbours and chat with them – and most of them seem eager to help. I hope the enthusiasm will be kept up …

… I looked in at the shelter today, rain water has seeped in and it is now on a level with the top of the steps – we shall need a boat if we are to use it.

Jan 30th

The Dene firewatchers cannot get enough volunteers so they have to do 4 to 6 hours per night on patrol – good thing when conscription comes in for some of them … I phoned Laurie C and she still has the little baby to mind. They had a land mine at the end of the road Xmas week and another bomb in their garden so are without windows back and front and 2 ceilings down … Next Wednesday we are on from 2 till 4am the worst watch of all as sleep is out of the question. Bill has been asked to stay at the (Royal) Exchange on Monday and firewatch there. They are a group of 10 – and 3 paid watchers – an unlucky number I wonder?

Feb 2nd 1941

Today we had firefighting practice on the green in Rosslyn Crescent. I manned the pump and demonstrated with the hose – putting out the bomb and the fire on the supposed curtains. It is not as easy to use as one would expect – but I managed it. We hope to have another one soon with real furniture to burn.

4th Feb 1941
Tonight is our first watch with the alert which went at 7pm – we have had occasional bursts of gunfire and one or two 'rats' passed over but did not drop anything. The first quarter of the moon is up and it is icy again underfoot – I do hope nothing happens for most people around have not taken their pails in and of course the water is frozen. This afternoon I brought the sandbags in and stood them in front of the fire for they were solid – they must be loose before we can use them. I have a helmet (tin) in front of me as I write, the inside is like those used as crash helmets by the speedway riders.

Feb 14th
The shelter is full of water. We really must get it empty for insects are beginning to get in there and it will not be healthy for too long. The all clear went at 11pm.

ARP warden Basil Radford was on fire-watching duty the first night of the Blitz on Swansea in 1941:

Feb 19
I was making a model of a Lysander plane when the sirens opened up at 7.38pm. This was my night for firewatching; we went out in pairs, my partner was Prof. B Farrington who lived opposite. I put on my heavy coat, it is very cold. The Prof kept his side of the road and watched my side, particularly the roof and I did the same from my side. The sound of the German planes was soon heard and flares were dropped, the whole crescent was lit up. What an eerie feeling it gave one, one felt so exposed. Within a minute the incendiary bombs began to fall. A large number came down in our small sector and lit up the scene still further,

most of them fell in the roadway and gardens. I noticed one on a small tree which was soon alight. It seemed best to let them burn out since some might be explosive and dangerous to approach. Then the prof called out to me – 'there is one on your roof!' My heart sank into my boots. What could I do to prevent the house burning down? I went back into the house where my mother (aged 74), my sister and her young son lived. My sister and I went up to the top of the house to see if the bomb had come through – it had not. I then told my sister to get my mother and the boy across the road into the house of Mr Ireland who has a good cellar. Even this crossing of the road was dangerous as the HE bombs were coming down, but it seemed the lesser of two evils. By this time the stirrup pump had been brought into our hall … but it takes three to work a hand stirrup pump. I then went into the back garden to see if I could get a view of the bomb. At that moment two soldiers who were on leave jumped over the low garden wall and offered help. That made three of us, so the stirrup pump could be worked. We went up to the top of the house. It proved a difficult task, the bomb had not yet burnt through the ceiling. We tried to play a stream of water on it through the window. This was unsuccessful. Next we tried to throw a sandbag on it with no success. We had to wait until the bomb burnt through the ceiling; as soon as this happened it could be dealt with. The fire came through quickly in five minutes. The working of the stirrup pump was a very arduous business, the water had to be carried up from the bathroom on the floor below. We kept our bath full of water every night for such an emergency and it proved invaluable, we were able to fill the buckets quickly. During all this time the HEs were coming down and we continually flattened out on the bedroom floor, though little good it would have been from a direct hit. We got the fire out.

Densely populated and with industries producing military vehicles, weapons, fighter planes and bombers, Birmingham was a prime target for the Luftwaffe between August 1940 and April 1943. It was, after London and Liverpool, the most heavily bombed city in the United Kingdom.

Don Thompson, born in 1927, lived with his mother and stepfather in Hall Green, a suburb of the city. The purpose of the earlier raids, he was clear,

> was to terrify the population. The city centre was completely destroyed and there were no military value at all …
>
> … Morale was quite strong. The ARP wardens would visit every house and make certain that people were all right and we used to go into each other's homes for a cup of tea. We were always very conscious of the location of people in houses so you did not sleep in the bedroom, but sleep down stairs so that you would not tumble through the floors if a bomb hit. So Mother and stepfather were in one room and I was in the back room downstairs. And if you went out you always told people so that the wardens would not waste time digging for you if something happened.

The port of Kingston upon Hull was strategically important but was also a convenient place for German bombers who could not find their intended targets to dump their bombs before returning home. As a result, fewer than 7 per cent of homes escaped damage from raiders.

After the blitz on the town in May 1941, Phillip Chignell visited his friend Arthur who lived in the Charterhouse in the city centre, and wrote to his sister on his return:

> 27th May 1941
> Arthur is now living the life of a troglodyte … He has his bed in an underground dugout, where he keeps his books

and his wireless. He is safe enough there from anything except a direct hit ... I had a cup of tea with Arthur in front of the kitchen fire and every window was broken and out and every door open and uncloseable and half the ceiling down on the floor. Just the same in every room, broken pictures, broken furniture and glass lying about everywhere, things crack under your feet as you walk about and all the time you feel the house is going to tumble down on top of you. Whilst we were having tea an unexploded bomb or a workmen's blast went off quite close and the whole place rocked. Just over the garden wall is St Phillip's church, the rectory belonging to this church and the Alexandra theatre, all close together. A bomb smashed the lot up. The theatre with its very big spiral tower fell right over the vicarage. Canon Sedgewick, the vicar and a friend of mine, has not been heard of up to now. Mrs Sedgewick was rescued from the wreckage. It is only a few days ago that I stood at this very corner talking to Canon and Mrs Sedgewick. A barrage balloon had broken away from close by and the trailing wire rope had cut the canon's telephone wire ... Canon Sedgewick then told me that he had just returned from burying six people who had lost their lives in one of the raids. Well? Whose turn next? This is just what it amounts to.

... I went into Hull on the Friday morning and saw what had happened. The raid attack had hit the centre of the city very badly. It looked as though a big earthquake had occurred. Houses down in every direction. Streets blocked with masses of stones and bricks and girders and goodness knows what else. I never thought I should live to see such a sight. I went in on my bicycle. Time after time I was turned off my road and sent up a bye street to get to my destination how I liked, so long as I did not go along that particular road the policeman or the soldier was guarding.

... The latest idea seems to be to drop a parachute, it does not matter very much where it drops so long as it drops somewhere. As soon as it touches the ground or anything in the way of a building there is the devil of an explosion and every house in the vicinity is wrecked. A tank of oil is released and at once ignites and if that is not hell my imagination fails me ...

... Someday Hull will recover and live again. Just now it has received a knockout blow. This sort of thing was rather expected right at the beginning of the war, when it did not come we all began to think it never would come. Well. The same thing cannot exactly happen again. We are never likely to see the city burning again as it did that night. There is not the stuff to burn.

On 22 June 1941 Hitler attacked Russia and this signalled the end of the big Blitz over Britain.

From July 1941, the Luftwaffe tactics included what the British termed the 'tip and run' raids. These were fast, low-level daylight attacks by single or small groups of aircraft. The low level aspect meant that the bombs travelled horizontally as they fell and were more likely to travel through walls at ground level than penetrate buildings from top to bottom. This resulted in casualties having to be rescued from upper floors which were relatively undamaged. Tip and run raids could be very damaging to civilians and property, as this record of the war in Eastbourne, compiled from official sources by N.W. Hardy, and published shortly after, shows:

May 4th 1942

After nearly eleven months without a bomb we were beginning to forget there was a war on, or were we?

We at least were living the lives of almost normal people until suddenly, with only about ten seconds warning from the Local Alarm, the Hun swooped and once again brought death and destruction to the town. It happened at 1.52pm.

Nine ME 109s were seen approaching Beachy Head at about 19 feet above the water. They climbed to clear the cliffs, hedge-hopped across the Downs and swooped on the town. They dropped their bombs in widely separated parts of the town – hitting St John's church and setting it on fire, scoring a direct hit on the gas works, another direct hit on the station causing severe damage to a train and station buildings. Another bomb fell on the permanent way near Cavendish Bridge and also hit a train. The Cavendish Hotel was hit, causing severe damage and trapping people under tons of debris. Three houses in Willingdon Road were wrecked by a bomb aimed at St Michael's church. Other bombs dropped in the Coal Wharf and in Commercial Road, damaging business property. The raiders also used their machine guns freely and a number of locomotives were damaged. Fishermen in a small boat were gunned as the raiders flew out to sea and one man was severely wounded. The bombs, which burst at ground level, caused considerable damage over a wide area. Although this type of attack was terrifying in its suddenness, the public kept a high standard of morale. And the defence services performed their jobs with wonderful speed and zeal ...

Casualties: five dead; thirty-six injured.

This was the first of 17 such raids on the town, the last being on 6th June 1943.

6

NEW STRATEGIES

From February 1941, a new phase in the Blitz began: Admiral Doenitz, head of the German Navy, wanted the Luftwaffe's support in the Battle of the Atlantic. This meant that the Luftwaffe turned away from industrial centres and concentrated instead on British seaports.

One such target, Clydebank, has the unenviable title of the most bombed town in Scotland. On 13 March 1941, 236 Luftwaffe bombers attacked targets in the area. Most returned the following night.

Tryphena Nixon (née Hislop), a teenager and ambulance driver, lived in nearby Bearsden:

> It was after midnight when our first call came and we started up our vehicle and began the journey as ordered down to Anniesland and thence to Scotstoun and Clydebank, there to await further orders from police or air raid wardens …
>
> … As we progressed slowly along Dumbarton Road, almost every window on either side was shattered and each house had its curtains billowing out from empty window frames like spectres in the night waving their arms helplessly before the fires which burned within.
>
> These ghost-like arms seemed to cry to us as we passed, yet so few people were abroad – most of them tucked safely away (we hoped) in their air-raid shelters.

Rescue workers search through the rubble of Eglington Street in Belfast in May 1941. News of the first major raids on the city on Easter Monday and Tuesday was not widely broadcast. This raid was concentrated on the dock area of the city. *Courtesy of the Imperial War Museum*

James Hastings, the depute town clerk of Clydebank, shared the duties of ARP controller for the burgh with two other senior officials:

> I phoned into the control centre and was told that nothing out of the ordinary was happening and there was no need for me to come down to Clydebank. I had intended to go on to perhaps supper or something at the house of one of my friends who were with me and I left the telephone number of that house in the control centre so that they could contact me if necessary.
>
> I went on to this friend's house, no call came through, and I think it must have been the unusually long period of the barrage which made me begin to wonder if this was rather different from what I had experienced before. I seem to remember trying to get in touch with the control centre again, but not being able to.
>
> I could not find out what was happening because there was always a tremendous security clamp on any information about air raids unless from official sources, and I was speaking from a private telephone, and … deciding that it was perhaps time that I was getting home, and home to me at that time really meant the office because we were sleeping in the office most of the time.

As Hastings walked towards Clydebank, he noted:

> There had been very little damage that I could see, proceeding along Dumbarton Road, but immediately I got to the Clydebank boundary the whole scene was one of devastation.

Arriving at the Control Centre, he realised very quickly that services were overwhelmed:

Fires everywhere with fire-engines and fire-pumps standing by, many of them doing nothing because

1. many of them were without petrol
2. the water main on Kilbowie Hill had been severed and all the mains in the lower part of the town served by the Kilbowie Road mains were without water and the fire hydrants were thus useless
3. the fire-engines in the lower end of the town near to emergency water supply storage tanks near the canal had to use long runs of hoses, and the constant hauling of these among the tremendous piles of broken glass that littered the streets had punctured many of them until they were virtually useless

Added to that, blocked roads prevented service crews from other districts from getting through.

I decided to go to Bothwell Street in Glasgow to the office of the Petroleum Department, which I reached round about lunchtime.

The office was virtually empty – only a young lad and a couple of typists. I showed him my credentials and described the situation as vividly as I could, and asked if a load of petrol could be sent down immediately. He obviously had no authority and after a bit of bargaining I asked him to get in touch with someone in authority.

He did phone somebody and I've no doubt he did his best but the answer was that of all things I was to come back in the afternoon and ask for Mr So and So and he would no doubt be able to help me. This was merely another example of the sort of peacetime easy-going attitude that I had experienced from most of the government departments at the time.

I remember asking him to get this gentleman on the phone again and having a devilish barney over the phone but really I might as well have been talking to a stone wall.

In the event, I had the idea I might as well go down to the petrol company depot at Bowling but before I left Glasgow I remembered that I had heard of a petrol depot – somewhere in the Port Dundas area. I finally discovered it without much trouble, got hold of the manager, told him who I was, and what I wanted.

I've forgotten what the number of gallons was, but it was in hundreds of gallons and cans, a ridiculously high figure in those days of strict petrol rationing.

I'll never forget the difference in his attitude from that of the Petroleum Office people. He seemed at least to have heard that something had happened down at Clydebank because in five minutes I was out of the place with an assurance that there would be a lorry load of petrol down in Clydebank as soon as I would be there: and he was as good as his word.

I went straight back down and there was a lorry load of petrol in cans in half an hour or so thereafter; and we lost no time in getting it distributed among lorries, fire-engines, etc. that were non-operative because of petrol shortage. From then on, we had no trouble on that account.

Mary Haggerty was a child at the time living in the tenements of the town. The house across the road from her took a direct hit:

We realised we could not stay in the close, but where could we go? Round the back courts were stone shelters, but we always said we would never use them as they were only death traps, but it was all we had.

We went into one nearest our close, it was dark in the shelter, and we could hear the bombs falling. And I knew by the sound they were very near, and again one landed very close, there was a terrible bang and I swear our shelter went up in the air and down again – we never thought it could have done this and still stay in one piece.

It so happened that the shelter next to ours had been hit, and all the men had to go and try to get out the survivors from under the rubble, people had sheltered in the wash house and it was a mass of rubble, they were all killed …

… We went up our stairs, the staircase windows were out and the doors had been blown off all the houses … I remember we just stood at our window, I mean the wide open space that used to be our windows, and watched No.12 burn.

Friday 14 March, 1941

I remember as the day went on, how No.7 – it was a wide pend [a vehicle entrance from the street through a tenement block] which stretched to the street right through to the back court – started filling up with dead bodies.

The rescue workers were putting them there so as anyone who was worried about missing relatives, went to the pend to see if they were there. Thank goodness I did not have to do that.

… We did not know where to go, we wanted away from the tenement buildings which took quite a bashing on Thursday night and thought if a bomb falls near our street the buildings will collapse, for our close was in a terrible state, there was a crack right up from the close to the top flat.

My father decided we were going to Denny, as our house was in a terrible state we could not live in it. My mother who had died many years before came from Denny and we had some friends there.

By this time there was some transport put on to take people away, as most of the houses were uninhabitable. The people were in schools and church halls and the Red Cross were serving tea. Our close was declared unsafe and Agnes and me were not allowed up to our house to get our clothes, so we went to Nellie's house. Later my father persuaded a warden to let him go up to the house.

We lived two storeys up and he took out my trunk which was full of my things which I had saved for my house when I got married. He also took out my brother's radio-gram.

I do not know how he managed to get them down the stairs. That was two journeys he made up the stairs and the warden would not allow him to go back up. He left them in a park in Dunn Street.

We went to Denny and we were treated great by our friends, they made us very welcome, in fact two of them – Crissie and Oweny Grant – gave us their house and they went and stayed with her father. We could not have had better friends.

My father had arranged for a van to go to Clydebank, he was determined to get more of our things out as we only had the clothes we were wearing, but when he arrived at Pattison Street on Sunday, No.11 was a mass of flames. He said he just stood and watched it burning and the tears ran down his face. It must have been terrible to see your life's work destroyed before your eyes.

My father never had a home of his own after that for he died before he was allocated a house and all we had were the two things he brought out. I know he was thinking of me when he saved my trunk and he knew John had saved hard to buy his radio-gram and he risked his life to get them out.

... We lost our home and most of our possessions, but the Haggerty family survived the Clydebank Blitz.

The official report into public behaviour during the raids says that morale was good, and it paid tribute to the quiet patience of people arranging accommodation afterwards. The chief topic of conversation – and a crucial factor in maintaining morale – was compensation for war damage. It also noted that:

> There were no ladders from the top tenement landings to the high ceilings of Radnor Park tenements. The breakdown of water supply compelled the Fire Brigade and the Auxiliary Fire Service to confine their attention to the lower parts of the town.
>
> But with all this it remains the fact that, the people themselves by taking adequate preparations could have saved a half or more of destroyed Clydebank.

Nearly all the homes in Clydebank were damaged or destroyed. At the outbreak of war Clydebank's population was 45,000; after the Blitz it dropped to 2,000, although it had climbed back up to 32,000 in 1945.

Two months after the attack on Clydebank, on 7 May, Greenock, further along the banks of the River Clyde, was targeted and once again the homes of the civilian population bore the brunt. The report by the fire-master, A.S. Pratten, made on 16 May, noted that co-operation and reinforcements from other brigades had been crucial:

> In the very early stages of the raid a stick of high explosive bombs struck the Ardgowan Distillery and fired a warehouse containing about three million gallons of whiskey. A tremendous body of fire was almost immediately generated and, from this time on, the area was systematically bombed, many neighbouring premises being set on fire. The Fire service was powerless to control the initial fire, in the circumstances, and the situation rapidly depreciated as succeeding buildings were fired. The raid then became more widespread and a serious fire situation developed.
>
> In the early stages of the raid, the water mains were so badly damaged as to be useless for the larger areas of fire and

it was necessary to relay water from the harbours and from aqueducts at the back of the town ...

... The telephone service was of negligible value during the raid. Telephonic communication with the auxiliary station nearest to the main fire area failed completely at about 01.45. At about this time all telephones failed, to be restored and fail again later.

But overall ... The local Fire Brigade organisation stood up to the 'blitz' remarkably well. It was overwhelmed by the number and size of the fires which were started in so short a time, but the organisation did not collapse and when reinforcements started to arrive the issue was never in doubt.

The control organisation worked smoothly and well and was proved to be capable of dealing with an even greater raid.

A marked feature of the whole experience has been the ready co-operation and willingness to assist on the part of other brigades. In particular, the Firemasters of both Glasgow and Paisley, and the Regional Fire Brigades Inspector, have been most helpful and this has had a decided effect upon the problems facing the local service.

In preparing for the bombers' return the following night, lights were placed a few miles outside the town and were mainly successful in directing them away from Greenock.

As the largest port area on the western coast, Liverpool and Birkenhead were subjected to regular and heavy raids – more than any city apart from London. This letter was written by Kathleen Hanlon, most of it while she sat in the family Anderson shelter ('The Dive'), to her mother in the Isle of Man. The shop she refers to, where she worked as a dispensing chemist, was in the Scotland Road area of Liverpool, about 2½ miles away.

The Dive
Thursday
Dear Ma,
Thanks for the letter. I nearly got my ticket to 'Kingdom Come' tonight. Have just landed home after a most exciting time. I had just left the shop when the sirens went & the guns started almost immediately & then I heard Jerry. I kept on walking however as there were no shelters near, & was just going up the Valley when – whistle – bang on my left & whistle – bang on my right & Chadwick Mount church seemed to go up in the air & come down all round me. It was so sudden, nobody had a chance to take cover. The trams were stopped immediately and everyone turfed off them, but he dropped no more near us. When I had recovered, I discovered that the church was still standing but not a window was left in it, the bomb must have dropped at the back of it. The blast blew a man over on the other side of the road from me & rocked a tram a few yards ahead of me. (There's the 'all clear' 8 o'clock.) A house in Kirkdale Vale got the 1st one, & there was a white powder all over the road, don't know what it was. About a dozen wardens came flying along & started banging at all the doors to see if the people inside the houses were OK. I heard someone shout 'burst the door open', that must have been the house that was hit, it hadn't collapsed, so it must have got it at the back. I hope I never get anything closer than these two, gosh, I was scared.

Kept on walking like Felix & discovered a fire in a house off Walton Lane, flames coming out of the windows – must have been an incendiary. Jerry was still buzzing round but I kept on the move & managed to get to Cherry Lane when the guns started full blast. I turned down Cherry Lane & tacked myself on to a man & the two of us trotted along as far as the Hermitage when we decided it was a bit too hot so we stood in the doorway there until the guns cooled off a bit. There is a mobile gun here which runs round the roads & it goes off with a terrific crack, not a bang, & it was busy near us. Then we decided to do a hop to the shelter by the Ebenezer, so we took to our heels & flew along the Drive among the bangs & flashes, the sky was just lit up. The shelter was full when we got there but we squeezed in the doorway. I wasn't there long before things went quiet & I made another hop home. I can't realize yet that I'm still in one piece. It was an awful experience …

… Hope you don't mind the bad writing & all the mistakes, but I guess my nerves aren't quite steady yet, & I'm in the house now, (Auntie Mag & I came out of the Dive when the 'all clear' went, but she has gone back now) so I'm listening to every sound outside even though there's no raid on.

I wrote to Pa on Monday night & told him that it had been pretty quiet here lately. I had hardly sealed his letter when Jerry dropped two time bombs which sounded very near here, but turned out to be in Gt Mersey St & Boundary St. One of them went off with an awful bang about 3.30 am & wrecked a Methodist Church. Another bomb scored a direct hit on a church school in Fonthill Rd behind Stanley Hospital. I went along & had a look at it on Tuesday night. It's just a heap of bricks & rubbish.

That umbrella shop in Clayton Sq., which was wrecked has a big notice outside – Demolition by Adolf Hitler & Co – reconstructions by Tysons.

That's all for now.

Love

Kath

Hospitals in cities vulnerable to air raids had evacuated many patients and staff but were still extremely busy dealing with the casualties. The Emergency Medical Service was a response to the shortage of medical staff these hospitals were likely to face when dealing with casualties of raids. John Robert Lee, an Australian-born surgeon and the author of the following paper, was 67 when he joined the Emergency Medical Service at the start of the war:

> British Medical Journal April 19th 1941
> EXPERIENCES IN THE RECEPTION AND TREATMENT OF AIR RAID CASUALTIES BY JOHN ROBERT LEE, M.D., B.S., F.R.C.S.
> These notes cover a period of two months when intensive enemy air raids occurred over London. During this period 227 patients came under my care and supervision. Many of us have seen and treated badly injured civilians brought to hospital as the result of road, railway, or works accidents in peacetime. It seems to me, however, that only those who have had to deal with victims of air raids can conceive the appalling condition and appearance of many of these patients on their arrival in hospital.
>
> A sight which must be seen to be appreciated fully is the almost indescribably filthy condition of many who evidently had been clean and well clad. A patient is brought to the receiving ward with her clothes cut and torn to shreds, her hair singed, filled with dirt, and matted with blood and cement dust, her body and limbs covered with grit and oil, her face blackened, bruised, and bleeding, her eyes, nose, lips, and ears filled with dirt, her head bandaged, and her limbs immobilized by improvised splints at the first-aid post. Truly it is a picture not easy to forget.

After triage, he describes:

> 'Our Routine'
> ...The patient was at once assured he would be safe and well cared for; those who were distressed because they could not

> see owing to dirt, swelling, or eye injury were told not to fear going blind. Their eyes were thoroughly cleansed and castor-oil instilled at once, and their lips and mouths were also cleaned. The patients then had a cup of fresh tea with sugar. Anti-tetanic serum was given to all the wounded. Brief notes were written and any such treatment was recorded on the case sheet, especially if morphine had been administered at the first-aid post. The patient was then sent to the ward. The nursing staff carried out their duties efficiently, often working on far into the night after a long day. Patients well enough were removed from the stretchers and put to bed.

After detailing procedures for pain relief, hygiene, anaesthesia, dressings, and the benefits of having two surgeons work simultaneously on any patient with multiple wounds, Lee describes the successful treatment of a girl aged 15, who:

> apparently had a large glass tumbler blown through her left shoulder …
>
> Her left upper limb was attached to her body by its vessels, nerves, and a band of skin about two inches wide.
>
> Her condition was desperate. The huge wounds in front of and behind what was her shoulder were filled freely with glycerin and iodine while resuscitation measures were being carried out. After thirty-six hours she was taken to the theatre and attended to as described herein. Portions of her coat and other clothes, with dirt and debris, were removed from the wounds, then more glycerin-and-iodine solution was constantly applied. Gas gangrene was feared, as cultures showed the presence of B. welchii. A dose of anti-gas gangrene serum was given. She did not develop gas gangrene.
>
> At the end of five weeks she was able to move her elbow, forearm, wrist, thumb, and fingers well. The wounds were almost healed, and her general condition was good.

> Many patients had literally scores of wounds on the face, body, hands, and legs. Excision was out of the question. These were treated by having the wounds curetted with gauze soaked in glycerin and iodine. On the face no dressings were used. The wounds were frequently painted. The small scabs were shed in about a week. Multiple wounds of the limbs were painted, and a sterile towel was placed so as to prevent contact with the bedclothes. All such wounds healed in less than a fortnight with very little scarring. By this method healing takes place rapidly under a scab with little or no pus, usually in less than a fortnight. There are no repeated painful dressings. The growing tissues are not damaged.
>
> The circulation and local nervous mechanism are not interfered with by bandages or other material placed around a limb. Every effort was made to avoid amputation, usually with satisfactory result …
>
> … Visitors were allowed freely, but were warned that there were to be 'no tears' while in the wards.

The blindness he mentions was a frequent if usually temporary problem. In May 1942, H.R. Clothier, by now in the RAF and stationed in Harborne near Birmingham, could speak from experience:

> We had raids regularly but there was one night that will always be remembered by me. The sirens had gone and the horrible droning of heavy bombers had started. Then came the thud of bombs not far distant, and then we saw incendiaries dropping in the gardens. We all rushed out to put them out and I totally forgot all my drills and tried to clout one with a spade. A great shower of light came before my eyes and I couldn't see. I fumbled my way indoors shouting out 'I'm blind!' Someone came and attended to me … and slowly I began to see again. It is wonderful to

> find that you have not been blinded and still have your sight. I shall never forget the relief.

With its extensive shipbuilding industries, Belfast was vital to war production. It suffered a massive raid – not widely publicised at the time – on Easter Tuesday, 15 April 1941. Over 200 bombers came over the city. More than 1,000 people died – the biggest loss of life outside London during a night raid. Half the city's houses were destroyed. James Doherty, an air-raid warden in the city, became one of 100,000 people out of a population of 425,000 who became homeless that night. He recalled later that the weather that day had been good and a German reconnaissance plane had been spotted flying over the city. At 10.45 p.m. the wailing sirens gave warning that enemy aircraft were approaching. The wardens who had stood by during the day were already at the post; others came hurrying in. Even those who had been on holiday and had scarcely time to unpack reported for duty:

> Suddenly the city was illuminated by giant flares which floated down on parachutes. How can I find words to describe the intensity of the brilliance which tore through the darkness and bathed the city in a light greater than the sun at noon? Every building stood out in detail and we could see in all directions. Royal Avenue, North Street and Carlisle Circus were plainly visible whereas a few seconds previously one could scarcely see an outstretched hand. The flares hung like giant electric lamps up in the sky. The flares themselves did not offer any threat to us but as we stood in the open bathed in their white light it was a disturbing and frightening experience. Frightening, because the city was exposed to the planes which could be hovering above like giant vultures waiting to dive on their prey. As I stood in the now fading light of the flares the thought came to me. Were

the blackout, the smoke screens and hooded car lights of any use? At that moment it appeared to me that they were all totally ineffective.

… Carlisle Circus and the Antrim Road showed signs of a heavy attack and my street was a shambles. What had been a row of neat terrace houses was now a mountain of rubble. I stood gazing at the mound which was once my home. I was dazed and frightened, thinking about my family, my father, my mother and sister … When I had spoken to them about taking shelter they often said that they would prefer to stay in the house rather than go to the shelters. Our shelters were far from being suitable places to spend a night. Doors were never fitted to them and they had lain neglected since they were built. Local residents used them as places for dumping rubbish and throughout the city they were often used as public conveniences. Overall they were dark, evil smelling, airless dungeons. Knowing the general feeling with which the public regarded the shelters only increased my panic. In a daze I made my way to the post, almost afraid to hear the news I so much wanted to know. I met some wardens who assured me that my family were safe … The more active of us decided to form a type of flying squad to investigate the various sites of damage and do what we could for the injured or partially trapped.

… Our plan was simple; we would move from site to site, treat the wounded, effect any possible rescue with our picks and crowbars and attack any fires which we thought we could control. It was a hit and run operation but we had to achieve something in what appeared to be a hopeless situation … Burke Street had disappeared; not a house was standing. The death toll here was high, as it was in this entire area. Everywhere we went we met with death, and the horror of it all was that the dead outnumbered the injured. I knew these people well and I had often chatted with them as I passed through the streets on patrol and the children would share their sweets or walk along with me. Now it was heartbreaking to think of their mangled bodies below those mounds of rubble. This was the hardest part of the warden's job … As I came in contact with manifest panic and fear, I was glad and thankful that I had become involved with A.R.P.

After two hectic days:

… we made it back to the post about 2 o'clock in the morning. My feet felt as if they were cut to pieces. I asked someone to pull off my boots and I lay down on the floor and fell fast asleep. I woke early, feeling refreshed. Others had joined me during the night on the floor and some were sleeping on the benches. It was a comforting sight. I was proud to be a part of this group of great fellows. There was no gas and we made a fire with sticks, and brewed a pot of tea. Someone produced a piece of bread. It was stale, but we spread it liberally with jam. There was no milk to be bought and what we had was sour, so we took the tea black. It was a rough breakfast but it suited the circumstances. There were at least a dozen of us living at the post. Our families had gone away or our houses were destroyed or badly damaged. I knew I would have to get some clean clothes and a bath and a shave. I could not go through another day in my present state. We went out on an early patrol. It was about 7 o'clock and as we moved through the streets the locals greeted us. Other wardens had kept contact with them during the night and like ourselves they did not go to bed but just dozed off sitting in their chairs. It was good to see them looking so settled and not frightened. The first night in the ghost town had passed quietly. On our return to the post I decided to go down to the old house and make a determined effort to rescue some of my clothes before the day really started. I was joined by about six or seven of the gang and we moved off like a squad of navvies carrying ropes, picks and shovels. The upper storeys and staircase had collapsed but I located what I thought was my bedroom in the heart of a mountain of rubble. The whole row of houses had collapsed like a pack of cards when a parachute mine exploded at the rear in Lincoln Avenue. We started to clear the debris and the gang worked as if a life depended on their efforts. The idea of digging for my clothes and other belongings was great fun for them and excitement grew as we unearthed the wardrobe and a chest of drawers. As they saw it, they thought of it as digging for buried treasure. The wardrobe and drawers were twisted and broken but I was excited and relieved as we pulled them out; but then sadness struck me. This was all that remained. This was all I possessed. We carried them to the post, which was to be my home for the next two months until I was able to get a place and bring my family together again. At the time I did not think much of it but later when I settled down in my new home my thoughts wandered to my books, stamp collections and a rare and beautiful collection of postcards and autographs of a grand selection of European celebrities in pre-war Europe. I was a keen Esperantist and I collected many small mementos from all over the world. Fellow Esperantists sent me autographs and stamps, some rare, some ordinary, but they all helped to build up a very picturesque collection which I treasured ... The Nazis did not approve of the Esperanto movement and its idea of peace and brotherhood. Hundreds of Esperantists were executed or disappeared into concentration camps. I lost some personal friends in this way. I never met them but a close friendship had grown up between us.

Now stationed in Worcester, Mollie Wilson was anxious for news about her parents who lived about 50 miles from Belfast.

The newspapers carried little information about the Belfast raid, so rumour was rife, as Mollie Wilson's letters show:

> 7th May 1941
> ACW Wilson
> c/o Guard Room
> Rudloe Manor
> Box,
> Worcs
>
> Dearest Mother and Daddy
> (4.20 am)
> I haven't heard from either of you for some little time now, and am just a bit worried in case the latest raid over Belfast interfered with your routine in any way. Have you been called up for the Civil Nursing or anything Mother? You see, I have only heard second hand about the raid, and though I have tried very hard I can only find very little information about it. In fact, I haven't seen it in print at all. One of the G.P.O. men, knowing I was from Ireland, told me about it, and that it was very serious, with huge numbers of casualties. So that is all I know. If it is true you will both be very busy, so don't worry about me. Letter cards will be all right, or a post card now and then, till the emergency passes. But above all, please don't work too hard.

When she does hear, it is apparent that in the absence of official news her mother plays down the seriousness of the attacks:

> 10th May 1941
> Dearest Mother
> Your letter arrived yesterday just after I had posted mine to you. I hope you won't think me silly for beginning to worry. But after the raid so many people asked me so many times if

> I had heard from home, that they began to make me wonder. Everything is okay now though and my only trouble is that you may be annoyed with me for being a little panicky. I'm so glad the damage to Belfast was so slight. You see, stories over here get so exaggerated, and this girl back from leave said that the city was practically flat. So I'll tell her next time I see her.

Plymouth was among the cities whose residents were especially hard hit by heavy and frequent raids. Water, electricity and gas supplies would often be cut off and in the early days of the Blitz, it took longer to draft in help from other nearby towns and cities. Choc Steed was a typist working for HQ South Western Command in Plymouth during 1940–41. She and Roy (who was in the Royal Navy) were married in March 1941:

> After a week in Penzance we went to Dartmouth where we intended spending our last week [of our honeymoon]. On the Saturday morning we heard on the radio that Plymouth had had a very bad blitz on the Thursday and Friday night, so we packed and left straight away …
>
> We had been away nearly two weeks and when we returned, the church where we were married was nothing but a shell. I believe we were the last couple to be married there. The restaurant where the reception was held and the photographers' were gone, as was practically the whole of the centre of Plymouth. The whole town was devastated and firemen had come from miles around to tackle the blaze. Friends of ours who lived in Torrington in North Devon, 54 miles away, told us how they stood on Castle Hill and watched the glow in the sky over Plymouth, knowing that men from their families had gone with the brigade to help … People were going out into the lanes around Plymouth to sleep. Those who could spare the petrol took their cars,

> but others walked. Every evening hundreds of women and children could be seen walking along the roads. I took my Mother out and sometimes my Mother-in-law and sister-in-law came with us. We couldn't go every night – there wasn't enough petrol – but we managed three or four times a week. We left about 10.30pm and returned about 5am. We pulled the cars tight into the hedge and got what sleep we could. When we returned, my Mother would make us a cup of tea whilst I took the car to the garage – which was about half a mile away – and then we would go to bed for an hour or so before going to work. One night we were all in our cars, tight to the hedge, when suddenly a German plane appeared overhead and machine gunned straight down the lane. Fortunately no-one was hurt. It had been cloudy when we parked and we hadn't realised it was a full moon and that when it came out it would shine straight on us. We all moved across to the other side in case any more returning planes passed overhead but it was quiet for the rest of the night.

The Women's Voluntary Services (WVS) organisation had been founded in 1938, partly to help fill the gaps in places where the Women's Institute, Townswomen's Guilds and similar organisations could not meet the needs of local people after air raids.

Anne Lee Michell was a member of the WVS. Born in Highgate in 1908, she and her husband Frank Lee Michell (referred to here as Mike) lived near Wellington in Somerset with their daughters Sarah and Caroline (Toots). Mike was in the Home Guard as his diabetes prevented him from joining the army. Anne's wartime diaries include this account of her visit to Plymouth as part of the Queen's Messenger Convoys. These convoys comprised WVS members who arrived in lorries within hours of a major raid to help feed survivors and rescue workers:

Saturday 3rd May 1941
12.45 Babs rushed out and caught me to say [we're] to head for Plymouth to cook for and drive the Queen's Messenger Convoy for food. Rushed home to pack then drove to Plymouth with Babs, Mrs Langford and Mrs Walker. Found lovely blue and fawn vans on the car park in blitzed suburb of Plymouth and drove one to Tavistock where they're [parked] for night. Muddled gears and held up the whole convoy! Dinner at pub in Tavistock then long moonlit drive over Dartmoor and Ivybridge(?) where a relative of Mrs Langford put us up. Whole day completely unreal!

Sunday 4th May 1941
Get up at cock crow an hour earlier owing to double summertime. Lovely early drive to Tavistock, found the right way and did it quicker. Drove my van to Plymouth and did day's work stirring soup, cutting bread and butter etc. Whole affair is rather a muddle, no-one to organise work, masses of helpers doing nothing, etc. Convoy = 2 kitchens, 2 stores, 2 water carts, 3 canteens. Canteens go on distributing food around Plymouth but we were not sent. Drove back to Tavistock. Van's nice to drive now I am used to them.

5th May
Drove over Dartmoor so lovely in the early morn, frost in the meadows and moors all misty. Such a hard day's work today, never sat down at all. Got sent out with canteen amid frightful rubbish ruined homes, soldiers doing demolition very glad of tea – dust so awful. Could never have imagined such scenes – nothing left of whole streets but twisted girders and rubble. People so pathetic, especially the kids. Terribly tired by the evening but drove back somehow.

6th May – our last day in Plymouth, glad as I am, so dirty from the smoke of our Dixies, and stray incendiary from raid last night lit a smelly Dixie very nicely! Was sent out again and soon sold out of soup and food, so drove home through ruined Plymouth and saw most of it. Shall never forget these three days. Hoped to be relieved from Bristol but no-one came so had to drive convoy back to Tavistock as usual and come home from here. Got in at 9.30 dead tired longing for Mike but had awful row. He has had hypoglaecemia … as he forgot to take his sugar on Home Guard. Told him off, he furious and me too tired to care. Wot a day – prayed a bomb would fall on me when Huns come over!

Survivors hurry away from the devastation in the ancient city of Canterbury on 2 June 1942, the day after the city's heaviest bombing, part of the Baedeker raids. Teams of firewatchers on the cathedral's roof saved it from serious damage by clearing away incendiary bombs. Many of the city's other ancient buildings were destroyed and 115 people were killed during 135 raids on the city. *Picture by Fred Ramage, courtesy of Hulton Getty*

7

BAEDEKER RAIDS AND THE LITTLE BLITZ

By 1942 the Luftwaffe was concentrating its power on the war against Russia, and from February that year the RAF was gaining the upper hand over Britain. It had become obvious to both sides that the greatest harm was caused by incendiaries which could be dropped in their tens of thousands in a single raid and would cause massive damage by starting fires across the target area. On 28 March 1942, the RAF attacked the German port of Lübeck, dropping high explosives and incendiaries on the old town, which was mainly made up of medieval wooden buildings. The raid caused widespread destruction and left 1,000 dead. Hitler ordered reprisals against Britain's oldest and most beautiful cities in what are loosely termed the 'Baedeker raids'. One view is that the Baedeker raids were so named because they were thought to have been planned using a Baedeker travel guide. It was also reported that Hitler had said the raids would cause the Baedeker guide to Britain to be rewritten. There were two phases in the Baedeker raids. During the first phase, the Luftwaffe bombed Exeter, Bath, Norwich and York. Canterbury was the target in the second.

Lily Pearson lived in York and was caught up in the Baedeker raid on the night of 28 April. After the raid she moved to a temporary address outside the city, from where she wrote this letter to her aunt:

Dorothy & I were alone in the lounge when the raids came. The first thing we heard was the siren, then incendiary bombs dropping on the back bed. The bedroom was immediately on fire, & we turned on the bath taps, got buckets to throw water on the fire and ourselves, until we were soaked, but the flames were out. The bombs however were still under the bed, which is a low divan, & is too heavy for us to turn over. We had to act quickly I assure you. We went downstairs, it was blowing a gale outside, all York seemed to be on fire, flames & bombs were everywhere. We put 3 out in the front garden, & 3 in the street, then called 2 soldiers to help us with the bed. They put the whole bed, mattress & all, through the window, where it remains, a burnt wreck, & then we put the bombs out with sand. By that time the big bombs were coming down all around. My brother Raffael was out, putting fires out, with the rest of the men & the soldiers who are billeted in some of the houses. It was just like a nightmare, they dive bombed us, & machine gunned, the house was frightful. We stayed in the kitchen, being the smallest & safest place, while the whole place rocked, while roofs crashed & glass, & houses were hit all round. Raffael saved 2 houses from the fire, & we saved ours, but the nice crescent is no more. Huge fires engulfed whole houses. About 16 people, all acquaintances & some friends, were killed round about. About 5 houses out of 15 remain & they are damaged. Raffael's is like ours, roof mostly off, windows nearly all gone, including a lovely coloured one, & ceilings down. The bedroom, newly decorated, is burnt, & simply a mass of wet sand, & burnt rags, & walls splattered with molten metal from the bomb. We didn't get burnt at all, but we had to keep putting our faces in water, as the fumes & flames were choking. Other streets are almost as bad as ours, the whole half of the town right out of the suburbs is bad, there are thousands homeless.

We meet dozens of friends every time we go to York from here, who haven't a stitch left & only borrowed clothes. Everyone is helping everyone else though, & we had a good stock of clothing and all kinds of things from the American Red Cross, & bedding for hostels for the homeless, & I can assure you it is very much appreciated. Our house was untenable, & I had offers of homes from quite a few places. Meanwhile Bert, in the nursing home, was, with the other patients, taken to the underground shelter. They had fire bombs on the roof & time bombs in the garden, but otherwise safe. He was very worried about us though, until we went along early next morning. We decided as Bert was due to leave, to come here to friends, so they brought him out by car. We are 8 miles from York, & it is so peaceful & quite lovely. River & woods round about, & Bert is getting better quickly. The roof is already back on our house, but we shan't return yet. I feel I couldn't go back for a while. The street is roped off as traffic would shake what remains. Only a few people are living there, it looks so desolate & horrible. We can stay here just as long as we like, but shall go back sometime I expect … street, Guildhall & station caught it badly. Penley's Grove street was quite untouched I think. We are so looking for the end of the war. I do hope you won't come any nearer to it than you have done so far. I pray that you & all your family will keep safe through it all.

I will write you again soon with all news from here, & I hope you will get this one anyway.

Once more, very many thanks for my 'Readers Digest'.
With love to you both
from Dorothy & Bert
& myself,
Your loving niece,
Lily

RAF raids on Cologne on 22–23 April and Rostock on 23–24 April are thought to have provoked retaliatory Luftwaffe raids on Canterbury on 31 May, 2 June and 6 June 1942.

Pam Cleverley (née Jordan) recalls the effect the Canterbury raid had on her life:

> In 1942 I passed the scholarship to go to Simon Langton Girls' Grammar School in Canterbury and in June of that year we spent the night in our Morrison table shelter listening to the blitz on Canterbury. One of the buildings destroyed was the school to which I was supposed to go in the September. For the first term we shared the boy's school building which was untouched. One week we went from 9 am. until 1 pm. and the next week from 1 pm. to 5 pm. It was a half hour bus journey from Herne Bay, which was fine until the cinema in Canterbury showed 'Gone with the Wind' and the performance ended just after 5 pm. which meant we couldn't get on the buses until about 6 pm. No mobile phones then, very few phones at all, so our parents must have worried. In January 1943 we finally found accommodation – the local psychiatric hospital. The patients had all been evacuated to Devon. As you can imagine the premises were not very suitable and the first few weeks must have been a nightmare for the staff. Directly you closed a door it locked, so the janitor spent his entire time rushing round with the master key. We had great fun jumping in the padded cells, until the head had them locked.
>
> I spent the rest of my school days in this building as the school was not rebuilt until 1948–49 after I had left. It was thanks to the dedication of the teachers that most of us had exemption from matriculation, when you consider that they lost all books and equipment at a time when they were irreplaceable. We had odd desks and books from surrounding schools.

In 1942 Mollie Wilson was on an RAF station near Bath:

> On summer evenings, when German bombers came droning over, thirty, fifty maybe in formation, we stood in the open gazing up at the black crosses on their wings, watching while one or maybe two of our own few aircraft took off to intercept. Sometimes our boys would shoot down two or three, before they crashed themselves, outnumbered and outmatched. German and British planes would spiral down together in a trial of smoke. For weeks, our half completed camp was strewn with wreckage hauled in by salvage crews and you mourned for boys you'd known who died that day.
>
> When Bath itself was bombed, civilians came streaming out, taking refuge in the village where we had our billets, sleeping, many of them, in the hedges, deeply shocked, unwilling to return. Bath was an 'open city', full of treasures, and they'd taken it for granted the war would never reach their very door. Surprisingly, the bombers never found our camp or never touched it anyway, but after a while, when things were going badly for the country and secure communications were absolutely vital, they built an operations complex down more than a hundred feet in caves that stretch halfway to Bristol. Hours were long and hectic, and it was part of our job to pass on air raid warnings, yellow, purple, red. Attacks were plotted on a large map table and you estimated threatened areas in an arc around the planes, advancing with them.

Other raids, all on East Anglian locations, are sometimes included under the Baedeker heading, but Lowestoft and Great Yarmouth especially were heavily bombed during the war.

The USA had come into the war following the bombing of Pearl Harbor on 7 December 1941. By the following summer, combined British and American air forces flew frequently over the East Anglian coast on their way to attack occupied Europe. Tom King, still on regular duty at his ARP post at Southwold police station, just up the coast from Lowestoft, noted the local response to all the activity:

> 31st July 1942
> Spent the morning in the garden and had a good sleep in the afternoon. Quiet day – a few planes. Heard on the wireless today that the Germans went to the Midlands last night and we brought down 9. Came on duty at 21.30 it was quiet up to 00.30 then our planes started to go out and it turned out to be one of the largest concentrations ever to go over to Germany. The noise got you a bit at times, you could hardly hear oneself speak, then at 1.00 they started out from the sea and kept up until 3.45, a series of explosions that vibrated everything, doors and windows vibrated as if they would come off their hinges. And nearly all the Boro turned out, about 20 different people phoned up to ask what all the noise was about, the noise ended about 4.00 but although a hectic night, we had no sirens. Came off duty at 8.00.

Born in America to an Irish-American father and English mother, William Joyce was brought up in Ireland and came to England in the 1930s, where he joined the British Union of Fascists. He went to Germany in 1939 and from there he broadcast weekly programmes to Britain on behalf of the German Propaganda Ministry, aimed at lowering the morale of the civilian population. Lord Haw-Haw was the name given in Britain to several broadcasters from Nazi-run radio station *Reichssender* Hamburg, of which Joyce was the best known. The broadcasts always began 'Germany calling, Germany calling' in an upper-class tone. British government requests that people should not listen had little effect but neither, for that matter, did Joyce's broadcasts significantly affect morale.

Roy Clevely, aged 11 when war broke out, was an only child living with his parents in the Redfield area of Bristol:

> I can always remember my father liked to try and tune into Haw-Haw crashing the BBC News. It could have been 9 o'clock or 10 o'clock – he was frowned upon a little bit for being pro-German but that was not the case, he was just interested in what Lord Haw-Haw, as he was called, had to say …
>
> Haw-Haw's mother used to live in [the] Fishponds area of the city and he knew the city very well …
>
> I remember him telling us 'the Luftwaffe would be visiting Bristol before very long' and naming all the streets – Castle Street, Mary le Port, Denmark Street, you name them he had them. And he said, 'Bristol you will be losing your famous …' whatever and lo and behold on the first blitz the very centre of Bristol was taken out, it was as accurate as that. We knew a great deal of it was false but when Bristol caught it, it was absolutely true. And later it came out that as early as 1936 they (German airmen) were flying over Bristol and other cities and photographing them.
>
> As a young boy I castigated him with all the language I could think of. Morale stood up incredibly well because in times of danger I really feel that the human spirit tends to rally and coalesce and I feel that the citizens of Bristol – of course very divided politically, in all shades, really did come together and there was tremendous self help and mutual help that occurred and it helped us to get through those dangerous times.
>
> Of course we always listened to Churchill's speeches. I suppose we wanted to see both sides of the story. We knew that the German propaganda was just that – a great deal was false but when they went for Bristol it was spot on. [Churchill's speeches] were tremendously uplifting and the

> man gave us tremendous hope and we used to doubt him at times – another country has fallen, prisoners taken and so on. [But at the] time we had this tremendous faith and confidence in him and in the coalition government.

Bristol was raided from 24 November 1940 to 11 April 1941. During that time, F. Wilfred Willway, a 34-year-old doctor, worked in Bristol Royal Hospital, where he was also ARP officer. As well, he was part of a visiting team helping in hospitals in Bath during the Baedeker raids of 25 and 26 April 1942. With his apologies for his dogmatic and personal style, he wrote to the *British Medical Journal* at the end of that year, offering his observations on the way arrangements for such assistance both helped and hindered hospitals in bombed towns and cities:

> In the winter of 1940–1 Bristol received its average share of air raids. I was active in all save one of these and learnt first-hand lessons. As the winter of 1941–2 approached we were all keyed up to face the bombardments that never came.
>
> Instead raids were made on smaller neighbouring towns, notably Weston-Super-Mare and Bath. It is obviously possible to view a raid on a neighbouring city with considerable detachment.
>
> Such vision may be useful, and I had the good fortune to assist in the 'good-neighbour policy' in all these raids. In each case we spent part of the time in the 'blitzed city' and part of the time organizing in the 'rescuing city.' This was possible as the raids were repeated on the second night in each town. On the whole the good-neighbour system worked well, but it is felt that many improvements could be made … Admittedly some of it is painfully obvious, but most British cities found that it took actual bombs to drive the lessons home!

Communications

... In the case of the Weston raid, phone communication with Bristol was good though the line was sadly overworked (raid excitement) and messages were repeated unnecessarily – for example, a request for more sulphapyridine was separately phoned up by four officials.

In the Bath raids communication was bad. (This is written in terms of the hospital personally visited.) I arrived there, at 2 p.m. on the day after the first raid. (I was then leading a surgical team under orders from the Group M.O.) We saw cases and operated till 12 midnight, staying at the hospital for the second raid. At 4.45 a.m. casualties were again arriving. Since leaving Bristol we had been unable to contact Bristol or the other Bath hospitals. The sole contact was the visit of a dispatch rider at 4 p.m. on the first day. We had then been there only two hours and were in no position to know what extra help might be needed, as the problem had only just been surveyed – e.g., some 60 casualties in an unfamiliar hospital with facilities for two teams to operate. At that time we were not au fait with the laundry position or the drug and dressing position.

At 6 o'clock on the morning of the second raid I returned to Bristol in my own car to obtain further aid. Clearly this was wrong. It should not be necessary to detach a surgeon to act as a dispatch rider. It is now obvious that when the dispatch rider called at 4 p.m., the aid I should have requested was the honour of a further inspection at, say, 10 p.m., when we would have understood the situation better. We should then have known enough to appeal for rations. The large team I brought was deplorably fed, yet it worked for 24 hours except for a 4-hour break, and most of its members had been up and doing in Bristol for 14 hours previously. Good warm drinks and substantial meals are necessary for the nurses, doctors, and others in such circumstances.

When Should Help be Sent?
The hospital in the bombed city may be cleverly organized, but it will need help.

If it is so staffed that it does not require help in an air raid, then it is over-staffed and is wasteful of man-power, and doctors should be requisitioned from it for military service! ... In one city that was helped – on the arrival of the rescuing team the whole resident M.O. staff of the hospital retired to bed – a sensible manoeuvre.

What Type of Help Should be Sent?
I have firm views on this subject, and they conflict to some extent with E.M.S. authority as stated in the 'Red Book.' However, I will venture to dogmatize.

... The 'Shock Troops' Team:
The first help to be sent should be strong parties of medical students with a few sensible housemen. These I consider my shock troops – they are 'go-anywhere-do-anything men.' They will give a blood transfusion, take a blood pressure, shave a head, write notes (vital: I have seldom seen a 'General' write a note), put out a small fire, act as stretcher-bearers, give simple anaesthetics, form a minor surgical team, and generally do the ten-thousand-and-one things that 'proper doctors' seem to find beneath them. The supreme pull of the big city over the smaller is not in the greater excellence of its consulting staff but in the number of its medical students. Where possible I would include in the shock division that other salt of the earth, an almoner with her clerk. This division, warmly clothed (Battle dress for shock troops is old clothes, a torch, pencil and pad, and a pair of dressing scissors) and well fed, should be on the road within 1 hour of news of 'the incident.'

... Surgical Teams:
The surgical teams that seem to be so beloved of the E.M.S. can well leave at a much later hour, say breakfast-time. They

are not needed in the first few hours unless the stricken area has no surgeon at all (highly improbable), in which case a surgeon must leave with the shock troops. Most casualties can well do with a few hours' rest; the few 'vitally urgent' cases can be dealt with by the local surgeons, who, having withstood the night's raid, will appreciate relief at 9 a.m. to see to their own homes, etc., but who do not want relief at 5 a.m. or 6 a.m.

... The wise surgeon will pack his own kit; every surgeon will have his own fancy, but in air raids the best surgeon is the one who needs the least tools. I have a passion for taking razors (and a student to hone them) and nail-brushes ...

It is well to carry goods for one's own comfort – e.g., a theatre suit, gum boots, and a mackintosh. The visiting surgeon who bothers the visited hospital for these things is not helping – he's wasting time, energy, and tempers. Ideally, a surgical team should be relieved every 8 to 10 hours, otherwise efficiency will fall off.

... Nursing Relief:

This is important, and requires nice judgment and execution. A two-nights-running air raid is a heavy test of the usually busy, usually under-nursed general hospital. If to the admission of numbers of casualties be added minor bomb damage (windows blown in, no black-out, etc.) and noisy excitement in the daytime precluding rest, then the strain on the night nurses is heavy. We tried the experiment of exchanging units of nurses between the central city and the bombed town, thus providing a 'quiet night'. This needs much arranging and nice timing when all hospitals are working full out with minimal staffs. Two experiences in practice are related, and are instructive:

Twenty nurses were sent at 9 p.m. to the Weston General Hospital after the second night's raid (obviously no one knew if a third night's raid would occur). These nurses were

> courteously received and were distributed among the wards; during the night the local nurses were each given 4 hours off duty and their work thus lightened. Had a raid occurred the augmented staff could easily have shared the work. (A similar exchange of house-surgeons is desirable.) A similar party of 20 nurses were sent to another hospital, where the matron had already been advised to expect them. They were met on arrival, told they were not wanted, and sent back crestfallen to Bristol. What a lack of imagination and tact! The hospital in question did not even notify this action to the A.R.P. organizer, with the result that next day a bus was sent to fetch back nurses who had been returned the night before! These contrary experiences merely confirm the need for good planning.

In 1943 a new type of device, the butterfly bomb, was dropped by the Luftwaffe. Henry Beckingham recalls:

> The two half cylinders of the casing formed a pair of wings to slow down their descent. The two end sections formed a propeller, the rotation caused the steel cable to turn and hence to turn the spindle which screwed into the fuse. When the spindle had been unscrewed approximately four turns the fuse was armed. Once armed the bomb could not be disarmed.

A large number of butterfly bombs were dropped on Britain in a raid on Grimsby and neighbouring Cleethorpes in June 1943. Although Grimsby had endured many raids during the conflict, there had been relatively few casualties until that point. This raid resulted in ninety-nine casualties, many of them children who mistook the bombs for shrapnel and picked them up.

Joyce Pomorska, then aged 14, was at a cinema in the town:

My father had gone out as a special constable and he didn't arrive home until very late, about ten o'clock in the morning. He told us about the bombs and that things were rather difficult and some people had been killed and he had to go out again. Well I had promised my mother to take her to see Yankee Doodle Dandy at the cinema and he warned us that we might not be able to get any transport but we did and we went to the cinema and we saw the film only to discover when we'd left that four seats away from us was a butterfly bomb. Fortunately there was no-one else in the row.

It was on the floor. I thought it was a light on the ceiling but apparently it wasn't it was a slight hole where it had come through. But nobody realised at the time what they were and practically every street was affected.

... My father took me and showed me [them] at the station. People had been bringing them in in baskets.

Well of course nobody realised that it was a dangerous thing to do and they were very fortunate that not all of them went off.

Bomb disposal teams were taking no chances. Henry Beckingham wrote afterwards:

There had been a heavy air raid on the 17th/18th August '43 in the Hull, Hedon and Hornsea areas, when a large number of butterfly bombs were dropped causing havoc. For weeks we were still searching in the hedgerows and ditches for these lethal fragmentation bombs. In many cases we had to resort to placing straw in the ditches and setting fire to it so we could clear the thick entanglement of undergrowth.

In Wembley, Rose Uttin was still fire-watching with the Fire Guards, who were as essential as ever in preventing incendiaries from starting major blazes. As her diary shows, not everyone was as diligent:

> September 3rd 1943
> Today starts the 5th year of the war. How much longer? Last night we attended a firewatch meeting. Now we come under the new fireguard order which begins on Sept 20th. We had preliminary instructions and commence new training etc very shortly. We must have pails of water ready as our supply coming from the Colne Valley via Watford makes us at the end of the main and should that be hit we shall be in a quandary.
>
> Sunday 31st October 43
> … We had a fireguard practice this morning, one section all turned out but some did not trouble so we expect to have another practice next Sunday morning – a fine way to spend a Sunday, preparing for this …
>
> … In our exercises we had a 'bomb' in our front room and one in Mrs Bradburn's hall to put out. I rushed and got Mrs Kneebone's stirrup pump and we practiced with it. A case of the nearest to hand with me. Connie Alcott ran the messages for Bill who is the group leader and knows what to do through his City practice. One group failed to turn out so the leader had to let his 'fire' burn out and that would have meant in the real raid that the NFS would have had to have been called out.

Operation Steinbock, or the 'little Blitz', as it was known in Britain, was launched in January 1944. The targets were mainly London and south-east England. Hermann Göring put the newly promoted Generalmajor Dietrich Peltz in charge of the operation and told him to avenge mass bombing raids by British and Allied forces, by now taking place day and night over Germany. Rose Uttin recorded the first raid of this new phase in her diary:

> January 21st 1944
> Three years ago we were sleeping downstairs in the lounge and worrying every time we heard a plane go over. Now we go to bed and if we hear any noise listen for a moment and then go off to sleep … 8.30pm warning went and fires started over London. We stood at the back door until the local guns started and then came inside. It got so heavy we sat under the table – for the windows shook so I thought the glass might come in. All clear at 10.15 and so thankful we were to hear it. Raid was very bad; incendiaries etc at Wembley Park and Alperton on the Fox film studios. Vans going round telling people not to touch any bomb pieces they might find.
>
> Sunday Feb 13th
> Tonight we had just finished supper, it is so dark out – I had to wait until I got used to the dark before I opened the side gate – 2 pails of water on the step. Am sitting writing this with the guns going off and my tin hat on – we are so sick of it all. Dora had gone to bed but as it got heavy about 8.45pm she got up again. Here we all are grouped round the dining table ready to dive underneath it if anything heavy starts.
>
> Friday 18th Feb 1944
> We have just passed through a nasty sharp raid started 12.45 and all clear has just gone 1.45. It was like the Battle of Britain days. I got up at once and dressed and Bill followed – very heavy gunfire and incendiaries dropped in the road – explosive ones as there was so much gunfire we did not go out for a minute but I stayed on getting water as the pails outside were frozen. Bill got the pump and went down

Castelton to a house that had one incendiary through the small bedroom – the people had just got up and downstairs as it came through the roof. It split the wardrobe and did a lot of damage but thank God no-one was hurt. Big fires in London right the way across – the red glow is still showing. How much more are we to have? 4½ years of war and we get so weary of it all. A big incendiary exploded about a minute away right by the pillar box and uprooted the tree but as it wasn't near the houses we just had to let it burn out. From the noise overhead there must have been a lot of planes. As the bombs whizzed through the air we three – Mother, Dora and I – crouched under the table, I was scared and went dry with fright.

One HE fell in the park, blowing up the children's pond – another fell in Clarendon Gardens – two houses down an old lady and gentleman still in bed were blown through the floor with the bed but got out and lost everything. 16 were killed at Blackbird Cross and lots of fires – all clear at 1.45 everywhere. Harold came in to see if we were safe as he heard it was our way.

Sunday 20th Feb

Still they come over – raid started 9.30, all clear 10.35 – not so many over us as Friday but fires are over London and lots of incendiaries fell – we just got under the table as they passed over – no sense in taking risks. We heard that Mrs Stevenson in Clarendon Gardens had two broken legs – the third house has to come down. We didn't feel so bad this time.

Monday 21st Feb

Whitehall was hit last night – Kensington and Park Royal amongst other places – Such a shock today, Mr Bradburn has passed away suddenly. He was on the gunsite at Hampstead when it was hit and the strain was too much for him. Poor dear what she has had to put up with the last 3½ years – first her son then her husband.

24th February
Raid last night started at 10.15 – just as I had been in bed an hour – so came down and endured misery for ten minutes. This morning we went to the canteen to hear that four parashooters had been brought to Wembley Police Station – quite lads, about 18. It has been funny to hear the tales that have been going round, one would think that hundreds were about. Raid started tonight at 9.40 and ended at 10.50 – terrific gunfire so we sat under the dining room table shivering and had a nip of whiskey. Many planes flying over but we didn't hear anything drop near like last Friday.

March 14th 1944
Once again I write – not of the Fire of London but Wembley. It started at 10.30pm and the swine kept diving low till he could see he had reached his target. When Bill and I got on the step what a sight. The factories were all aflame fully 150 yards into the air – thank goodness the railway is between us and the fires – although the houses in the road must be burnt out as well. I cannot write anymore – I feel too upset as several nice girls I worked with were on night shift there. (added later: 4 factories burnt out)

For much of the United Kingdom the Blitz was over but Tom King's diary shows that the East Anglian coast was still experiencing regular raids. Lowestoft and Great Yarmouth were regular targets for the Luftwaffe throughout the war:

Saturday Jan 29th 1944
Heard several German planes and scores of searchlights went up, had no incidents locally, but plenty of planes. The

Lowestoft barrage went into action at once, had the all clear at 21.35, quite a long warning. The military on exercise put up plenty of flares which made the civilians swear; quiet night after.

Training exercises were part of daily life. In April, he records one which went disastrously wrong:

22nd April 1944
Came on duty at 08.00, fairly quiet day not many planes about in the morning but several big forces of bombers in the afternoon, also fighters. No warnings during the day, came off duty at 19.00.

The police specials had an exercise tonight with the Home Guard. There is supposed to be an enemy landing. Crowds of planes about in the evening, they went out at 18.30. Planes returned 21.30. Beattie and myself went out to look at them, hundreds of planes were coming in and dropping red flares, made a very pretty sight but I was tired and went to bed. I'd not been there two minutes when the siren went 22.09 and heard m/c gun fire. Got up and we went outside. Saw a plane in flames to the north of the town, looked like a parachute flare going along, then it dived to ground and went up in a sheet of flame. Just before I came out another plane, a Liberator, had gone down over the town on fire and crashed at Girlings Farm Reydon in marshes near Quay Lane. Some of the crew baled out, five were found injured. One was pulled out of the sea by coastguards and Captain Clark of Coastal Battalion; the other four came down on the common and marshes. One dead airman was found at Walberswick and two were found near the plane at Reydon, so 8 were accounted for and two missing from the crew of ten. Had another plane on fire over the town, it crashed just out of our section, near Kessingland – damn. It seemed as if planes were crashing everywhere. What had happened, German planes had followed ours home and when we were dropping flares the planes made a sitting target. I heard about eight planes were shot down. One of the crew told us they never dreamt there were any enemy planes near. We had a hectic time at the Report Centre, many conflicting reports. White for red came through at 23.12, then a big force of our planes went out, and a second warning 23.21 and white 23.42, third at 00.30 and white 00.41 and 4th white 4.45. I went home to bed at 01.00 and never heard the last siren. We had no more incidents.

'Scalded cat' raids were a relatively late feature of aerial warfare. In these the tactic was to launch a short, sharp, high-level raid in which a few fast planes would drop their bombs and quickly head off before anti-aircraft guns and civil defence sirens could swing into action.

In his record of the types of raid on Eastbourne and their impact on the town, N.W. Hardy noted that scalded cat raids took place during the last two weeks of March 1944. This was the first of them:

March 14th
Three hostile planes of the fighter bomber type crossed the coast near Langley Point in moonlight with engines shut off. They glided over the town, released their bombs, restarted their engines and headed for home. One bomb hit the station and severely damaged numbers 2 and 3 tracks and the station buildings. A second bomb exploded in Hartfield Square, severely damaging house property and setting fire to a number of Army trucks, jeeps and motor cycles. The third dropped in the sea off Langley Point.

Casualties: one slightly injured.

By 1944, WAAF Betty Bullard was stationed at HQ Transport Command in Harrow:

22nd February 1944
Air raids for the past five nights. It's all a little wearing. Sunday was the worst – the siren went at about 11.30 and the barrage is so noisy and things begin to shake so much that I dig out my slacks, collect a greatcoat and tin hat and go and investigate. It's all rather alarming and I am distinctly frightened: guns are terrific, incendiaries spatter down in the square, a bomb which fortunately doesn't explode whistles down on to no 17. We stand about in the hall while the fire guards rush about with buckets and cluster on the steps outside ready for a call from Mrs P who is on duty on the roof. I move a few buckets vaguely and get rather in the way. I look out of the front door to find fires all around, the post office sorting office is burnt out, so is Stewarts hotel behind Pantings. The occupants of the UXB house are evacuated on to us and everyone is most efficient. They are taken into the drawing room and I pour out tea for them and offer my bed to some of the poor old dears who really need it, but they refuse so I supply my eiderdown and lend an MTC girl, who incidentally knows Pam, my dressing gown. I make myself some coffee, hot up my bottle and go to bed about 2am.

Another raid last night. I stay in bed until I decide I'm really too frightened to stay any longer. Descend to the hall and talk to Mary and Rachel, Mrs R and a small black kitten, an orphan of the storm, and immediately feel much better.

Have offered myself as a fireguard as I feel I really ought to do something. Had to confess my ignorance of exactly what one does but they were nice about it. Nice story. Fire party ordered out to a fire when they got there told it was too big for them, leave it for the NFS engine. Up comes 2nd fire party, unknown to 1st, rushes in and extinguishes fire. Enormous indignation of 1st party.

28th Feb 1944
More raids, in fact every night until Saturday. Lots of fires on Wed. Went on the roof with Mary after the all-clear and could feel the heat of a house up the road where the top floors were blazing and the roof had fallen in. NFS got it under control very efficiently all in about 20 minutes. Miss Pepper and fire party distinguished themselves, they were called out to one fire, then on to another; two men overcome by smoke so they pulled them out, kept it under control till the NFS arrived and just got out before the roof caved in. NFS congratulated them and presented Miss P with the bomb. American soldier 'I think you ladies are wonderful, may I shake you by the hand?'

The Bromley centre Royal Observer Corps in October 1943. Initially a civilian volunteer force, the Observer Corps was formed in 1925. It was the only means of tracking enemy aircraft once they had passed over the British coastline. They warned of enemy aircraft approaching so that sirens could be sounded, and became the Royal Observer Corps in 1941 in recognition of their contribution during the Battle of Britain. That same year their numbers were increased greatly, mainly by the introduction of women of the Women's Auxiliary Air Force. *Courtesy of Imperial War Museum*

8

V-1S AND V-2S

By the time the Little Blitz ended, in May 1944, an initial Luftwaffe force of nearly 550 aircraft had been reduced to 329 bombers. There was, however, little respite. Even with few planes, the Luftwaffe could launch the short, sharp, 'scalded cat' raids before anti-aircraft guns and civil defence sirens could be activated.

New weapons, the V-1s and V-2s, launched from sites along the French and Dutch coasts, took up the attack on Britain. Despite their similar names, the V-weapons were very different.

The V-1 was a pilotless plane powered by a simple jet engine. It travelled at speeds of up to 350 miles an hour. When it reached a pre-set location, in all but the latest models, the engine would cut out and it would go into a dive. A few seconds later it would hit the ground and the warhead would explode. People soon recognised the low pulse of the engine, which gave rise to the nickname buzz-bomb. It was also known commonly as the fly-bomb and the doodlebug. The V-1s could be launched at any time of the day or night and, initially, anti-aircraft measures were ineffective against them. Soon 100 V-1s were being launched each day at London and many towns and cities within the weapon's 200-mile range.

The first V-1s fell on London on 13 June 1944. Hetty Long, an elderly widow living in Camberley, Surrey, wrote about the attacks to a friend:

Horsham
Sussex
July 25th 1944
I have thought about you and your friend and feared that those dreadful things would pass your way, and one can only pray to God to protect all dear friends from danger. We get many alerts and some nights are very disturbing, the nearest crash 2 miles away, 3 in the night, the floor shook. On June 15th I arranged to spend the night in London with my only sister, she lives at Streatham which had had much damage. We went to bed about 11pm and at 11.45 pm the first plane passed over, an awful noise from the engine, we got up at once, then the alert went and before we left the room, the explosion. We went downstairs quickly to the Morrison shelter, and remained all night. It was a dreadful night. The guns sounded as tho' they were right over our heads, on the roof. About 3am one passed very low over the house and almost before we could speak we heard the explosion. I thought it had hit my sister's house and really looked for it to collapse, but it had gone over the next row of houses and crashed on a house straight across from my sister's back bedroom windows, killed all the occupants, hundreds of windows broken, but in her house no damage, the doors and windows blew open. She had a good deal of damage in 1940, but it is a well-built house in the residential part. With my nerves not very good after the long strain of nursing my husband, I really was terrified, tho' she remained very calm, and so worried on my account, she thought I would collapse. The alert was on until 10am and the noise going on all night. It was the first night those horrible doodlebugs came over and I shall always remember it, and the alerts went on all the morning. I left on the 6.34pm train, feeling such a coward to leave my sister alone. She is a widow, [and] I begged her to come here, but she said if she left her house she would go

where there were no alerts. The nights became worse, and to my great relief she left London on June 20th to join her daughter and little granddaughter at Combe Martin. Her daughter has taken a flat there for the duration and I hope my sister will remain there. I have a mattress under the stairs, and when daylight comes, go up to my bed to rest; and sleep if possible. I feel so thankful that my dear husband has been spared this terrible time, greatly as I feel my loss, but my anxiety with his helplessness was almost beyond endurance when enemy planes were above us. These are indeed terrible days, and I do feel so sorry you have so many around you, and I am so thankful you are both safe. I have been alone all the time, as I feel no one would care to come to a danger zone.

Shortly after the first raids, Kenneth Holmes, a teenager living in north London, started recording his thoughts:

28.6.1944
I have decided to write this diary after 13 days of almost incessant air attacks on London by Hitler's much vaunted 'Secret Weapon' the 'Flying Bomb', since named by the public 'buzz bombs' and 'pilotless planes', later officially termed by the German High Command as V1s.

I will always remember the 20th June our fifth day of flying bombs. I was in the GPO in Tottenham Court Rd. when I heard a rumbling in the distance which sounded familiar as by this time I was becoming accustomed to the sound of flying bombs. But as the alert had not sounded I decided to ignore it. At that moment the bell rang in the building followed by the sirens, the PO clerk said there was 'imminent danger and they were closing' (and she wasn't joking). I strolled across the road to my employment and had just got inside the building when there was a tremendous explosion which shook the entire building and threw me across the floor a matter of six or seven yards. I picked myself up and found the room full of dust as though a terrific gust of wind had blown in. I thought my last hour had come. I went out into the street and saw a great pall of smoke rising further down the road, and decided to investigate. But what I saw I will always remember. The scene was indescribable, the bomb had crashed about 80yds away actually at the rear of Tottenham Court Rd police station, which is always thronged with people, they were wandering about in a dazed condition faces streaming with blood. Mothers with bandaged hands, legs and feet, covered all over in dust. A horse lay dead, a victim of the surprise attack, shop windows completely blown out and shattered huge lumps of masonry some smeared with blood, and glass scattered everywhere, ambulances speeding in both directions, civil defence workers already searching for victims. Civil and military police including American moving the sightseers onwards, American soldiers were even helping the rescuers in their work which gained the admiration of all onlookers, including myself. Many lives must have been saved by this prompt action of the authorities and the speed with which they worked in typical London fashion of getting on with the job, as I was on the scene within 3 minutes and found the various organisation, military, CD and police all busily engaged. And even our great American ally seemed to welcome the opportunity of being able to render assistance. I thanked God I was safe and uninjured, though a little shaken. The average Londoner took it well though many said they would prefer the Blitz bombs to these weapons. I believe people are beginning to see that it is going to be longer than they had anticipated.

V-1s were also a common sight on the east coast, where Tom King recorded sightings in his diary:

1st July
I was doing a little gardening in the evening about 19.40 when I heard a noise like a traction engine from a plane. At once thought it was a Fly Bomb. Out at sea I could see a small plane going along at about 200ft up and flying north. I went to RC and phoned through to the coastguards to ask if it was one, they said they did not know. At 19.50 we had a red through with white 20.00. We then had a report from coastguards that it was a Fly Bomb and it landed in the sea east of Kessingland. I never heard an explosion, I don't believe there was one. This is the first Fly bomb we have had pass the town. I hope we don't get any more.

14th Oct
Had a warning at 19.53 when I was on duty, it was fairly quiet at first and then all the guns opened up on a Fly. I looked outside, just as I got there a shell hit on the Fly, there was a terrific flash of orange flame followed by a hell of an explosion, glass fell everywhere about 300 houses, 57 shops, the church and two chapels were damaged, fortunately only one person, a soldier, was slightly hurt by shrapnel. We had a busy time at RC [Report Centre] there is a hell of a mess in the town. It was good shooting by the heavy and light AA [Anti-Aircraft]. I believe it was the light that got it down.

6th November
At 20.16 we had a warning; 8 Fly Bombs went past the town and six were shot down by gunfire. I saw 5 of them explode. They were all south and just out of our area. The searchlight at Easton came up several times, one Fly crashed on landing in the Minsmere area after having its tail shot off, white 21.01. Crowds of our planes came back at 21.30 and the guns opened up on one of them but missed thank God.

Jeanne and Marion Thompson were 13-year-old twin sisters living at Salmon Street in north-west London. They recalled later:

> Of course, at that time, we were not allowed to venture far from home except to go to school and back, so when the summer holidays of 1944 began and six empty weeks stretched ahead of us, we decided to make up all sorts of games to play and keep ourselves entertained. One of these was tracking the flying bombs as they came over our house and recording them in a log book. We divided the day into fifteen minute periods of 'watch', each sister taking her turn to listen out for a doodlebug and writing it in the log.
>
> On July 21st 1944, the first day of the school holidays, we took up our positions diligently, ears pricked and pen in hand. Between 8.15 and 1.30pm we recorded 30 but we had no time at all to note the thirty-first for, as it passed above the house, the engine cut out and we knew it was about to come down. Our mother, who was in the kitchen nearby, ran in and grabbed us and we piled into the small cupboard under the stairs. As the bomb hurtled to the ground, the noise was deafening, like the rushing of an express train, ending with a huge bang. At the time, we were sitting on top of a lot of bottled fruit which had been stored for the winter and all the lids of the jars flew off, covering us in bits of fruit and juice. The cupboard door jammed and we had to force it open. When we managed to get out into the hall, a scene of devastation met our eyes. The front door of the house was halfway up the stairs and there was dust, glass, smashed furniture and ornaments everywhere. Although our house had not been directly hit (the one opposite was totally destroyed), it was very badly damaged and not liveable in, so, after a night at a local rest centre, we left for our grandmother's home in the north of England where we stayed until April 1945.

Measures to combat V-1s directly included anti-aircraft batteries, barrage balloons and fighter aircraft. Tracking the V-1s presented new challenges for the Royal Observer Corps. Eric Wilton, a member of B Crew of the Observer Corps Centre in Bromley, Kent, outlined the procedure:

> On the long-range board a cluster of red-dotted plaques fringing the coast of Kent shows that we shall not have long to wait before the next wave of raiders comes in. Jerry loves to time his attacks to a schedule and you can normally bank on a good big salvo somewhere around 11 o'clock. These plaques indicate radar plots. Somewhere in the gathering darkness of the English Channel nine evil shapes are streaking low across the calm water; and in a hundred operations rooms, on aerodromes and gunsites and in Observer Corps Centres, by this miracle of science, their courses are being accurately charted and plans laid in good time for their destruction. Already the fighter patrols that constitute the first line of defence are taking their toll. A plotter takes down a plaque from the long-range board and calls to the Duty Controller above: 'Diver 101 removed'.
>
> Now the first plaque has moved inland. Maidstone's posts have picked up the tell-tale light from the flaming propulsion duct. From now on it's up to the Observer Corps.
>
> … It takes the doodle bug no time at all to cover the few short miles between the coast and Bromley's boundary … Diver 104 seems to be coming our way. Roger 0373. Queenie 8985. That line will bring him bang over the centre. Already the heavy throb of his propulsion unit, with its curious overtone of urgency, can be heard clearly above the noises of the room. Queenie eight seven eight five: the noise is deafening now. There is only one thought in the room, though no one betrays it; suppose he cuts … Some day if this goes on, one is bound to cut at the right, the unlucky place

… the walls vibrate. The air in the room seems to throb. He must be terribly low. Sometimes they don't cut. Sometimes they just dive headlong with the engine racing …

… This was not after all, the one …

… While Diver 104 has been monopolising so much of our attention three other flying bombs have been moving across other parts of the table, and a fourth, caught in the vast balloon barrage some six miles south of Bromley, has exploded in mid-air. Within a few minutes, all these raids have run their course. Out of nine indicated by radar, five have reached the table. The other four presumably have been shot down by guns or fighters on the strongly defended coastal belt. Four out of nine, plus one caught by the balloons: not a bad bag! Week by week the number of radar plots that do not reach the Bromley table is creeping up.

Harry Atterbury, a teenager who had left school the year before, was having a lie-in:

On a quiet Sunday morning after a warning had sounded and after I had promised to leave my bed to follow my parents who had left the house to take shelter in the brick street shelters, a V1 crashed at the corner of the street about 200 feet away. My parents' home was completely demolished with me underneath. I was still alive because my bedroom door had been blown inwards, twisted in the air and had somehow fallen over the bed, resting on the top and bottom bed frames, creating a space in which I was saved from being crushed. The door held the debris off me. I soon regained consciousness, choked with the soot, dust and smoke; terrified by the noise, shouts and screaming. My reaction was to struggle and shout until I suddenly noticed a chink of light to one side above me through which I eventually pushed my hand. This action led to a frantic effort to get to me by some rescue workers who had seen the movement and I was pulled out quite naked and bleeding from the numerous abrasions caused mostly by flying glass and scratches from jagged wood. I had a coat or blanket put round me and was carefully carried in the arms of one of the rescuers, up and over the debris of my home.

At the same time I saw my mother and father framed by what was left of the front door jambs, standing crying and in a state of shock, hardly believing that they could see and hear me again. After they had been assured that I was not seriously hurt, we were led through the smoking rubble and past so many people tearing at and digging into the ruins of other houses, where other people were still buried.

Whether it was reality or not, I still remember seeing the head of an old lady who had lived next door lying on top of the ruins of her home and I believe detached from her body. Another horror came when after a few yards we stopped, whilst a couple of the rescuers removed the boots from two legs that were protruding from the chaos of broken bricks with the intention of putting them on me. At that time I did not know that the legs were artificial and belonged to a man who had still not been rescued; knowledge of that would not have made the situation or nightmare any easier for me.

We were led to the underground station at Essex Road where there was some emergency help offered. Word was sent to my sisters, who were living at Stoke Newington and we were soon collected by them. We went to the home of my sister, Ada, in Hackney. Over the next few weeks I returned to dig in the debris of our home although there was little left to recover. But on one occasion, two/three weeks later, when raising up the corner of our flattened kitchen table, I was startled and horrified when a filthy, stinking lump of fur moved and I took into my hands our old pet cat still alive. On the bus to Stoke Newington so many other passengers expressed sympathy for her, even in that filthy state. She lived with us for several years after, until the day she was killed by a car.

During those days, my older brother, Alfred, was rescued from drowning when the landing craft on which he served as a gunner was sunk during the Normandy landings. He was not informed about the V1 that destroyed our home and only discovered this later when, after hospitalization, he was allowed home on sick leave. When he emerged from the underground station at Essex Road, he witnessed the sight of flattened and destroyed streets where his home had once been. One shock on top of another weakened his health so he never regained his vigour; this resulted in his early death just five years after the war's end.

V-2s were rockets that travelled faster than the speed of sound, so fast that it was impossible to warn of their coming. The first attack was on Chiswick on 8 September 1944. Kenneth Holmes was fascinated by the lack of official news about the new weapons he saw and heard around him:

Friday 8.9.44
As I was writing my diary tonight 6.45pm there was a colossal explosion (certainly the loudest I had heard) which rocked the entire house and shook the windows violently, followed by a rumbling for a few seconds, and then a softer explosion. I at once thought that Hitler's threatened 'rocket bombardment' had begun but no other explosions followed. I tried to get the idea from my head then I thought it couldn't have been a doodlebug because there were no sirens sounded and besides a flying bomb doesn't make an explosion as loud as that, I also doubted if it was a pick-a-back plane [some V-1s were launched from planes in mid-air] because of the fact that there was no alert. Well

what else could it be? More like a gasometer had exploded or maybe a munitions dump? I tried to think it was one of these but all the time at the back of my mind there was a doubt as I asked myself is this the beginning of a new bombardment for London by long-range rockets? However time will tell!

Thursday 14.9.44
I was awakened this morning at 5am by two more shattering explosions, both the explosions shook the house and rattled the windows. I was told later that the explosions (which I think are the enemies' long-range rocket shells) occurred at Walthamstow E and Dagenham, Essex again. I have been looking in every paper to see if there was any mention of these 'explosions' but there is nothing at all. Why are we not being told about these? Obviously security measures which convinces me that they must be rockets.

Betty Bullard's brother, Dr Edward Bullard, was Scientific Adviser to the Air Ministry and the Admiralty. As her diary shows, lack of information about the V-2s did nothing to prevent discussion:

15th September 1944
Teddy is advising Air Marshal Hill at ADGB on the rocket bombs that are arriving from Holland. They weigh 16 tons and travel faster than sound, go 55 miles up into the air and down again and cost £40,000 each! However, there's only one ton of explosives and not many have come over yet.

Morrison [Herbert Morrison, the Home Secretary] of course has not allowed anything to be given out to the papers yet and everyone is talking about mysterious bangs and 'gas mains' blowing up. 4 more doodle bombs this morning launched from a/c [aircraft] over the N[orth] sea.

Kenneth Holmes continued to track the explosions he heard around him and the coverage in the newspapers:

> Thursday 5.10.44
> More flying bombs were launched against London and southern England during the early hours of this morning causing damage and casualties. An alert sounded this evening at 8pm lasting about 30 minutes and there were two explosions in the distance. These headlines appeared in today's Daily Mail: 'Germans decide V2 has failed', 'Dutch based weapon too inaccurate', 'Atom bombs to be speeded up' (by the enemy).

The newspaper report he refers to was by Ralph Hearns, their war correspondent in Stockholm:

> Thursday 26.10.44
> There were two tremendous explosions early this morning followed as usual by the rumbling sound as if buildings are crumbling down – after the explosion. Security measures are very strict apparently as the public are not encouraged to refer to these explosions as rockets but are still being talked about as 'gas main explosions' which of course seems absurd, though obviously to prevent the enemy from knowing where these have actually landed. One of these landed near London Bridge railway station and the other at Clapham Junction. There is still no mention of these 'mysterious explosions' in either press or radio.

Mollie Wilson was by now stationed at Elstree in Hertfordshire, in a large house with several other WAAFs, when she experienced her first V-2:

> Crash! Our greenhouse collapsed, our windows shattered. The duty officer flew up the stairs with her Red Cross

box and someone put the kettle on for a late brew. Then suddenly, out of the blue, came a roar, a flash, and a second explosion, bigger and more terrifying, lighting up the sky. That was the very first V2 rocket. It gave you no warning at all. By the time you heard it, it was too late to worry. After a while we got used to these, too.

Meanwhile in Becton, East London, Betty Holbrook, an ATS radar operator on the London rocket gun sites in east London, was being briefed:

> One day all the Radar Operators were called together for a meeting. Something new was in the air. V2s had become a menace and the latest idea was to try and find out at what angles they came down and to fire in those directions and so explode them in the air. Normally, the Receiver was rotated in its search for targets, as only when directly facing a target could it pick up a signal.
>
> Now we were to do a 'watch' every night from 7pm to 8.30am, and for this purpose both the Transmitter and the Receiver would be lashed to a certain bearing, so that if any target were seen on the tubes, it would be coming in on that bearing; and directly at us!
>
> I was on the first watch with Joy and Joan. We went into the Receiver at 10pm and stayed there until 7.30am when we were relieved for breakfast. For this operation we did not need transmitter operators. Joan (our number one) wore headphones with a tannoy fitment. She had a stopwatch and a pad of forms to fill in. Every half hour a voice would come through the headphones. 'Synchronise stop watches! Five … eight, nine, ten and the time is …!' and Joan checked her stopwatch.
>
> We then sat and waited, sometimes talking, sometimes just sitting – but never sleeping. It was very difficult to stay awake.

But it was most important to stay awake, because when we had to move we had to move FAST! As soon as a V2 was launched from its site across the channel, Joan received a command, 'Big Ben! Big Ben! Big Ben!'

She repeated this to us. We then operated certain switches etc according to a specified 'drill'. We gazed steadily at the illuminated tube waiting for a target to appear. We knew that the target would be moving at a fantastic speed. As soon as the V2 crossed the coast of England we got the command, 'Alarm! Alarm! Alarm!' We watched even closer. It was not often that we did see anything, which did not bother us at all as we were very conscious of the fact that when we did, the 'thing' was coming straight for us!!

While we were gazing at the tubes, Joan would be receiving, 'Five … eight, nine, TEN!' So when there was something on the screen we had to record Bearings and Angles every five seconds. We called these out to Joan who recorded them on a special form which was taken to London by a despatch rider early the next morning.

As Kenneth Holmes' diary shows, V-1s and V-2s soon became part of daily life:

Sunday 5.11.44
Today I witnessed the nearest escape I have had so far, once again I thanked God that my family and myself were untouched though a little shaken. This morning very early there was another 'tremendous explosion' and yet another at 10.15am. It was about 5.15pm and I was slowly strolling down the road passing a street shelter when I saw a vivid flash just above me. Thinking it was lightning, as it was raining I took no notice but immediately after there was a tremendous explosion followed by the sound of breaking glass. I at once threw myself against the shelter (or was

I blown?) and covered my neck and face the best I could with my hands. At that moment I thought the end of the world had come. The earth trembled, the very air seemed to vibrate, my ears seemed to be deafened, and a buzzing sound was passing through them. I cannot adequately describe my feelings. I thought I was accustomed to hearing 'bangs' and 'explosions' but <u>never</u> have I heard such a deafening sound and it is surprising what one's ears can receive and remain normal. I didn't need telling the cause of this explosion and as it was the 5th of November, I realised instantly that this was one of Hitler's 'fireworks', be it a rocket V2, V3 or whatever else the German High Command name them. I was only a few yards from my home but I covered the distance in record time to see if my family were safe. I found my Mother and Father quite safe and Dad busy inspecting the damage and though no words were said to the effect, I sensed by the look on my mother's face, her relief that I too was safe. The table was laid for tea which of course, now would have to wait because the important job at the moment (to Dad at least) was to get the damage patched up temporarily and quickly before blackout time, which would be in about half an hour's time. The window frame had been blown into the room and here I would again remind you that the frame contains a white canvas substituting glass. Of the few remaining windows at the back of the house 6 were shattered, the locks had again been blown off from the doors, and though all this was most annoying, on a 'quiet Sunday afternoon' my innermost thoughts were for the more unfortunate victims (not far away), maybe killed, maimed or suffering untold agony under the debris of what was, a few moments ago, <u>their</u> homes, which gave me a feeling of thankfulness that at least we were spared. Here I must confess my youthful curiosity urged me to investigate. I didn't have to travel far, as 100yds away in a thickly populated area, ambulances were already on the scene and treating casualties. I saw several people suffering from cuts and bleeding, waiting to be treated (a miniature battlefield), houses I had known well, were just not there, and the debris appeared to be around the surrounding houses (what was left of those). Goodness knows where the houses that had been struck had disappeared to! It looked as though a huge bulldozer had lifted them from the earth and there was quite an open space. Other houses in the immediate vicinity were badly blasted and partly demolished, a sight with which I have become familiar, but never have I seen houses or buildings so cleanly swept away as I have already described, and here note most of these are 3 and 4 story tenement houses sheltering 3, 4 and even 5 families. Surrounding streets over an area of ½ a mile (including my own) suffered damage, shop windows were shattered and their goods lying on the pavement. I also noticed large pieces of clay scattered even as far as 300yds from the 'incident' which told me the missile must have struck very deep and to add to all this a heavy downpour, which must have hampered the rescuers. This is certainly the worst 'incident' I have experienced and I feel sure the casualties will be heavy. During the day we had three rockets.

Monday 6.11.44
More flying bombs were launched last night, a few fell over a scattered area and minor incidents were reported at a number of places. Today there have been no explosions at least none that I have heard. Digging is still going on (all day) today for people trapped in the incident yesterday (Boothby Rd, St John's Way N19). It has been continuing all through the night and today even as I write (9.30pm) the rescuers are working with the aid of searchlights. I have been told that in the house the rocket crashed on, there was a children's party in progress and there are said to have been between 25–30

young children at the party. Also two Alsatian dogs trained especially to scent and discover persons trapped have been brought in, these dogs have been used in many flying bomb incidents. I'm afraid the casualty list will be heavy because this is a busy junction and shopping centre where people queue for buses and these would most certainly become casualties. Had this happened on a Saturday it would have been more disastrous as the centre is a very well known shopping area, also the traffic is more busy then. There was also a bus and a tram blasted. Walking past the scene of the 'incident' today it indeed looks like a battlefield; glass is scattered everywhere, the fronts of shops blown in, shutters twisted and buckled, ambulances and police cars parked and many sightseers. It is indeed a terrible sight. I said a week or two ago that I hoped I would never get a chance to judge which caused more damage, a flying bomb incident or a rocket, now I have had my opportunity, from this incident and what I have seen, I personally think a rocket. During the day we had one alert.

Tuesday 7.11.44
... Rescue work is still carrying on in Boothby Road N19 day and night. I have been told the search is being made for the children as only a few have been found.

Wednesday 8.11.44
... I noticed today that the rescue workers had ceased in Boothby Rd N19 apparently late last night. People in the district say that not all the victims were rescued and many still lay dead beneath the ruins, some of course were even blown to pieces and will never be recovered. This does not make very pleasant reading but they are plain facts which should be placed on 'Germany's account'. I am sure the rescue workers did everything in their power to find the buried

and deserve the best of praise. I am told the casualty list is 43 killed, 83 hospital cases, and a 100-odd walking wounded which makes a total of 226 innocent civilians. I realise more than ever now that we are indeed very fortunate to be alive through God's mercy and had this particular rocket crashed a little nearer – this page would never have been written!

Today there has been the first mention of the V2 in the press – after two months of these 'mysterious explosions'. This is what I read: Berlin – 'V2 attack on Greater London Begun', 'Speed 1,000mph says neutral'.

'The German High Command announced this afternoon that V2 attacks on London had begun. In their daily communiqué they said "the area of Greater London has been under fire since June 15 with short interruptions and in varying strength ... The fire has been intensified for some weeks past by the use of a second and far more effective missile the V2."'

Betty Holbrook recalled how terrifying surviving a V-2 could be:

I was walking from the Transmitter to the Manning Hut, deep in thought, when, suddenly I found myself being rushed backwards, absolutely unable to help myself. The air around and above me was vibrating madly. I was horribly frightened. I was nearly back to where the Transmitter stood and was wondering what was going to happen when the TX and myself meet. There was a tremendous explosion and pieces came down out of the sky. I saw everything as through a rippling pool of water. For a second everything was quiet. The TX door opened and two came out, looking as amazed as I felt. We looked at one another and said together, 'Yes, it WAS!' And pretended to wipe perspiration from our brows. Pretended?!! That was a V2 exploding in the air. Just a few yards from where I had been standing, I found a big wheel-like thing full of marble-sized ballbearings. It was heavy: this was part of a V2. It was well and truly embedded in the ground. I was just a little shaken. But picked it up to keep as a souvenir, forever!

After that episode we never went around alone, always there were at least two together. This feeling of not wanting to die alone was very, very strong. Personally, my greatest horror was that of having one moment of intense fear; that of actually seeing a V2 or FB [flying bomb] sitting beside me for one part of a second before it exploded. This, I was sure, I could not survive!!

In Wembley, Rose Uttin was still on duty:

August 13th 1944 Sunday
Up to and including tonight – 56 nights of fire watch for us all in turn, a longer spasm than the Battle of Britain. We did have six weeks and then a lull but now the warning goes without fail every night at 11pm … we fireguards sleep in all our clothes at night except our shoes and top coats in order to be out of the house in the least possible time – it is two months now since we completely undressed to go to bed. After four years of being a fireguard we have been issued with navy armlets with the words 'Fireguard' printed on them in white – so far we haven't needed them. It is now 11.30 and I am going up to lie on the bed and get a little rest. Talk about turning night into day.

August 29th
Another day of buzz bombs Mrs Cooper and I went to the canteen morning and afternoon (WVS). Just as we were walking along the road the klaxon went and a neighbour dragged us in to take shelter. It struck me as rather funny to

> get under a shelter in midday and I felt like giggling, so did Mrs Cooper. We stopped long enough to hear it drop – and then politely thanked her and went off again.

Anti-aircraft measures and the capture of launch sites by British and Allied forces curtailed V-1 and V-2 attacks, but they continued to bring death and destruction across the country right up until the end of the war.

9

CLEARING UP

There were fewer raids by the Luftwaffe after the failure of Operation Steinbock and so the blackout was less important. From September 1944, even though V-1 and V-2 attacks continued, civil defence services were wound down and, except for a 5-mile strip along the coastline of the UK, the blackout was replaced by the dim-out.

As her diary shows, the relaxation in regulations did not meet Betty Bullard's expectations:

> 22nd September 1944
> The Dim Out is disappointing as practically none of the street lamps are working and everywhere is practically pitch black and grim. Got to have some kind of curtain and the only thing most people have is blackout. However I don't put up the shutters now except of course when the siren sounds which it has done tonight.

But as J. Grenville Atherton recorded in his diary, in Manchester the dim-out was greeted with more enthusiasm:

> September 1944 was a 'black-out breakthrough' as the lights were switched on again at night in Manchester and Salford. Various towns had consultations with the Town Clerk (Mr J.W. Trewas in Stretford), the Chief Constable, and 'Lighting

Superintendent' (grand title). On Tuesday 12th September, 1944 I joined hundreds of sightseers in Manchester to see the street lamps lit. The Manchester Evening News printed photographs with the caption: 'the illuminations in St Peter's Square caused gasps of amazement.' For once the reporters got it right. There were shrieks of excitement and more than one person was seen striking matches just for the novelty. How different everywhere looked.

Mollie Wilson wrote to her parents about a trip to London with a boyfriend, John, on the last days of his leave from the RAF:

20th September 1944
Generally the dim-out has not been a great success but Boreham Wood has not managed too badly. In particular, I noticed a block of flats, with each floor a complete tier of light. They had, by accident or design – all their windows covered with orange curtains, a colour which certainly enhances the brightness of electricity in nights as dark as these we have now. It was like a fairyland after all these years, and I was completely fascinated. Some people, of course, do not bother with the new relaxation, because if a warning sounded, there is such a terrific flap – and, as you will have heard on the wireless, we do still have an occasional siren. Instead of shrugging their shoulders and carrying on reading or darning socks or whatever they've been doing, they have to trip about in the dark, struggling with shutters and things they can't see. No wonder they are none too enthusiastic, but believe me, if they knew how good the lights make all us homeless people feel, they'd endure even that …

… Walking along in central London … along the Thames Embankment. Eventually, just as it was getting dark, we disembarked at Charing Cross, and walked all the way along the Embankment, eating apples and flinging the cores into the Thames. You know, I have been terribly lucky. Always, I have dreamed of doing just these things, and there was little reason why my dreams should have come true. There are so many air force stations in England, and so many away from London. And yet we strolled along as though it was the most natural thing in the world. Silly, isn't it? We sat on a bench under the trees, watching light flickering on the opposite bank, and buses running across the bridges and either side of us. Everything was rather dimmed and muted by a soft, fine mist and London was very quiet. Trams passing behind us flashed lights on our faces and policemen passed swinging their batons. It was all so wonderful I could have stayed there all night – though it would not have been very seemly. We listened to Big Ben striking 8, 8.15, 8.30, 8.45 and nine, and just as I began to think I ought to be moving, what do you suppose? In a house behind us on the opposite side of the street, someone struck up Tschaikovsky's Piano Concerto. Remember the one I love so much … At about 9.20, we started back as I had come on night duty – and that was that. In a little while he'll be ringing me to say 'Goodbye' and I shall take up my visits to the Landergains or resume my dancing again, as though he'd never been.

For Rose Uttin, life was improving:

Monday Sept 11 1944
At last we are free from firewatching. The idea of going to bed every night without the thought of possible raids is wonderful to contemplate. Saturday the word comes through that firewatching is finished. It is four years since Mrs Bradburn and I kept watch on the steps – and I never thought it would last so long.

ATS girls operate a rangefinder at a 3.7-inch anti-aircraft gun site firing against V-1 flying bombs, 21 July 1944. The Auxiliary Territorial Service played a major role in Britain's anti-aircraft defences, working on mixed anti-aircraft batteries and searchlights. Efforts by anti-aircraft and the RAF to divert and shoot down V-1s were quite successful, though they had little effect against V-2 rockets, which travelled faster than the speed of sound. *Courtesy of the Imperial War Museum*

But the raids continued:

> Sept 30th
> Raids and doodlebugs on and off since I last wrote (11th Sept). Went to Winnie's yesterday and two warnings as soon as we got in. Another at 4.45 up and down, we are more than sick of it – war no nearer to being over than this time last year.

Throughout the war there were clear divisions of opinion in Britain, among those who experienced air raids, regarding the bombing of German civilians. V.M.H. Owen, leading Wren coder at Fort Southwick, wrote to her parents:

> July 9th 1944
> I have just been talking to another Wren about bombing – I don't know how it cropped up but she said she sympathised with the newspaper campaign in favour of our bombing Germany indiscriminately until they stop the flying bomb – in fact she thinks of bombing them to revenge their bombing us – don't you think that attitude is wrong – that it would be as much a confession on our side of failure and that we can't take the bombing, as it is on their side. Besides I don't think it would help shorten the war and would only do ourselves far more harm after the war that we lowered ourselves to their level – same as I still think it is a mistake for us to have shackled the prisoners to retaliate for their shackling ours – though I entirely see the point of view – but of course I have very little right to talk about it – never having seen a bomb in my life – but don't you agree with me?

Rose Uttin was of a very different opinion:

> Nov 9th 1944
> The second warning had just gone at 10.15 and we sit

> waiting. I feel somehow I could not bear to scramble under the table tonight and it is so cold the shelter would be intolerable. As I feel at the moment I loath and despise anything to do with the war and I am sick of thinking how we must 'sit back and take it'. Mr Churchill said that at the Mansion House today 'we must exert every ounce of energy tired as we are after more than five years of war' – tired is mild to what we really feel and we have to do 'the nice thing' for posterity's sake and the history books that will be written about it. Personally I don't care a dam what the historians write – for the fifth generation to follow – if they have any sense they will start their wars good and proper without observing any of the niceties that our government are doing now – in case they offend the Germans. I spoke to one woman in Lyons yesterday – her husband has been abroad with the troops five years and she was sick of everything.

In 1945 Kenneth Holmes, after reading a newspaper report about the last RAF bombs to fall on Berlin, commented:

> We living in Southern England cannot help but feel pity for the Berliners when we hear that 'our bombers were out over Berlin again last night.'

Constance Logan-Wright was a member of the London Executive of Bundles for Britain Inc., a US initiative that involved donating and distributing essential items to people who had been bombed out. This report followed a visit to those sheltering in caves in Dover – many of whom, as the war ended, had no other place to live:

> 16th November 1944
> Thinking that Bundles members might be interested in first hand news of Britain's front line town – Dover – Lady Beatty

and I went down there for the day last week. During the five years of war the population had dropped from 42,000 to 14,500. Many people had left soon after the outbreak of war but very many others did not leave till their homes were destroyed or made uninhabitable by shelling …

After lunch:

We then drove on to the largest of Dover's cave shelters. With 100 feet of sheer cliff towering over it, it gave its shelterers a wonderful sense of security and these caves have literally saved many hundreds of lives. The entrance is in space quarried out of the cliff-face in the days of the great sailing ships. These ships, having discharged their cargoes, were in need of ballast and the easily quarried limestone 'of the white cliffs' proved very useful. On the outbreak of the present war, the tunnelled cliff face was hurriedly extended into great long galleries radiating from a kind of central hall, and into these galleries were put three tier sleeping bunks. The shelter we saw could accommodate 2,300 men, women and children, and was wired with electricity throughout. It had a complete operating theatre and first aid post, independent water supply from deep springs within the cliff, kitchen, clothes and bedding space. Also it had sufficient food storage to feed all shelterers and staff for fourteen days if necessary. During the days and nights of heavy shelling it and all the other shelters were full to capacity, and even now that much of the danger is over, there are still nurses and other helpers on duty there night and day. 'After all', one of them said, 'there is still Dunkirk in German hands, you know and there is always the chance of a V1 or a V2.' Many homeless townpeople still sleep in the caves and we noticed many suitcases and rolls of blankets on the bunks, the property of modern cave-dwellers. Dover is certainly to be envied the wonderful protection of these caves and I could not help wishing Londoners had been able to burrow so deep.

From the caves we drove up to the heights of the cliff tops and there the Control Officer showed us the outlook posts manned night and day by wardens who watch the flash of guns on the French coast. The whole of the coast line was marked out in sections on a map and directly the warden spotted a flash, say in section 2Y, he immediately telephoned down to the control centre in the town and rescue workers and ambulances were ready to dash to that part of the town where the shells from that particular gunsite would fall.

In this way confusion was avoided and many lives saved. We talked with one of the outlook wardens on duty – a wonderful old man of 72 – just as keen and virile as a man half his age. He has taken regular duty hours from the beginning and told us he would not change his post for anything in the world. It must have been pretty lonely away up on that cliff top at night with shells falling round or screaming into the town far below – just two men and a telephone in that queer little hut buried up to eye-level in the earth. And yet one could understand his pride.

As we were waiting for our train back to London, the stationmaster said with a grin – 'well we've been through some strange nights and days and we've often wondered just what would happen next – but here we are. Now our one idea is to put everything to rights again as quickly as possible.'

Well – good luck Dover – we hope your troubles are over and that now the big tidy up can begin.

Many people were still in need of a place to live, as well as the most basic items, as Constance Logan Wright's report of a later visit shows:

29th January 1945
Mrs King and I have been down to one of the Rehabilitation Centres run by the WVS in a district which has suffered most from rocket bombs recently. Here victims of Hitler's visitations come for clothing and household essentials such as a tin kettle, saucepan, brush, blanket (one of the latter is allowed for each member of a family) and here today, for the first time, some of the cretonne chair covers you gave were being given out. When we arrived there was a long queue of old men, women, and children outside the large temporarily roofed-in hall. Inside were long tressle tables piled with the quota of gifts which were to be handed out today. These gifts were so precious that they have to be very carefully allotted and each recipient has to hand in a card on which has been written official details of damage their home has suffered and their most urgent requirements. For instance only those with a chair or a sofa left would be allowed to take one of the covers – those whose homes have been destroyed and who are living at the Rest Centres would have to wait until they had a home to go to. There was great excitement over some of our Bundles blankets – they were gay lovely things and naturally everyone wanted such a bit of bright colour to cheer up their blitzed home. I was so surprised to see these blankets, knowing that you have not sent any over for many months now – but it was explained that these had been held for emergencies in many parts of Britain and are now being released for all the areas suffering from rocket bombs. They gave the recipients the greatest joy and many recipients had tears in their eyes as they went away. So too with the patchwork quilts made from coloured pieces of flannelette – the brighter the colour the more precious they are because they help so enormously to decorate a dingy paintless room.

Further down the hall were tables covered with china teapots, little vases, jampots, plates, spoons, knives, and forks, bits of looking glass, soap dishes, etc, just about anything one needs when <u>all</u> one's belongings are gone. These things had been sent in by towns and villages in the 'safe' areas of England. Most had already seen good service, but since they are all difficult to buy new, they were eagerly snatched up. Quite a lot of framed pictures, photographs and texts have come in from the same source. Some of the latter we felt had not been very well chosen, one in particular, 'Prepare to meet thy God' was perhaps not the most encouraging text one could select for people who are every day and every hour in the 'firing' line!

V-1s and V-2s continued to cause havoc across the country until the final days of the war. The last V-2 to hit Britain came over on 27 March 1945, and the last action of any kind against British civilians occurred two days later when a V-1 landed in Duckworth, Hertfordshire.

Ann Maxtone Graham, who had been living in the relative safety of Market Harborough, returned home to London:

The two houses directly [to the] back of us had been removed by a bomb. The garden wall had fallen in, which made a horrid mess. I had opened up all the windows carefully and thoroughly, and not one bit of glass was broken. The whole window frame in the nursery bathroom had blown loose and hung down from the top, but the glass was intact. The shoring up I had had put up in the basement passageway was removed. We did a little painting and a little wall washing, and then it began to look almost human. I can't remember how I found a builder to do all the odd jobs, but it was a minor miracle, for everybody wanted someone to fix their houses in any way possible. On the workmen's last day I came out of the kitchen (now our living room) with a broom in my hand to speak to the foreman, who was getting ready to depart.

'You know, I'm not very happy about this ceiling,' I said. 'It looks a bit shaky to me.'

'Shaky, Madam, no, sound as a drum,' and he took the broom out of my hands and gave it a good bang with the end of the handle, whereupon the whole thing came down on our heads.

As the war drew to a close, Choc Steed also returned home, to Plymouth. On 3 July 1945, while Roy was in Australia still serving with the Royal Navy, their son Keith was born:

Keith was christened on 31st October in St Andrew's church where Roy and I were married and he behaved very well! Perhaps I should say that he was christened in the ruins of St Andrews as the church was just a shell then, but has since been rebuilt. Roy came home on 25th February 1946 and we were a complete family at last.

Tom King was part of the coastal defences and so was still hard at work even in these last days:

Wednesday 2nd May 1945
Had two months notice today from CD duties which we finish on July 1st. We seem to have had a good run so I can not grumble. The part-timers finish altogether from today so it seems the war is over at last. Crowds of planes about all day, still on supplies for Holland, also had notification today that the siren finishes today at 12.00. We have had 2,046 warnings since the war started.

Betty Holbrook's time in the ATS was coming to an end too:

One of the points we brought up was that none of the ATS who had been on the site for two years was entitled to a Defence Medal. We just had not been in uniform the three years necessary to apply for one. We all knew people who had never even HEARD a civilian air raid warning but because they had been in uniform for three years they had got a medal! We remembered that Sir Frederick Pile, the biggest man in ack-ack, had visited the site and told us face to face that the girls on anti-aircraft on operational duties were the cream of the ATS. BUT NO MEDALS FOR US! We had also heard that Sir Freddie was trying to get a special medal for London Anti-Aircraft people. What a hope! So, NO MEDALS FOR US!

A nice memory was of us walking around an open market in the East End of London about the time of the 'Little Blitz' in 1943/44. We were in battledress, with our boots and gaiters on and wearing our sleeveless long leather jerkins; very spick and span with our red anti-aircraft flash on our sleeves plus the special radar flash; a red circle with white 'sparks' coming out of it. It was rather embarrassing, but we got a round of applause from the stallholders and their customers. Some cheered! Some of the male stallholders came out and kissed us on our cheeks and some of the women hugged us. 'Well done, girls!' We grew taller. Probably had tears in our eyes. 'WOW!' we said as we left. That was really something! Maybe they could keep their bloody medals!!!

POSTSCRIPT

Most of those whose experiences feature in this book survived the war; of a few, there is little information beyond the accounts from which I have quoted.

As peace came, the aim of 'getting back to normal' was uppermost in people's minds. Fortunately, many nevertheless kept their letters and diaries and reflected on their experiences years later, writing memoirs of what had been an extraordinary time for all who lived through it.

Ann Maxtone Graham was reunited with her children in 1944, although she recalled her eldest son, Peter's, resentment towards her for leaving them in America. She and her husband Pat separated in 1946, whereupon she returned with John and Michael, her twin sons, to the USA; Peter, after service in the navy, went east to become a tea planter.

Of the doctors who wrote about working through air raids, John Lee enjoyed several years of retirement. Sadly, Wilfred Willway, who knew he was terminally ill when he published his observations, died in 1944, aged 36.

When Phil Piratin wrote his memoirs, in 1948, he was MP for Mile End in Stepney. Another MP, Duff Cooper, became, briefly, Minister of Information in Churchill's cabinet and ended the war as Britain's ambassador in Paris.

J. Grenville Atherton, Harry Atterbury, Mary Baker, Cecil Beaton, Elizabeth and John Belsey, Vera Brittain, Roy Clevely, Pam Cleverley, Phillip Chignell, Alan Deere, James Doherty,

Leslie Gardiner, Kathleen Hanlon, Betty Holbrook, Mary Haggerty, Tom King, Claire Lowry, Anne Lee Michell, Joyce Pomorska, Choc Steed, Donald Thompson, Mollie Wilson, R.H. Lloyd-Jones and Muriel Simkin survived for years after the war.

Intriguingly, Betty Bullard's diary ends in 1945 just as she is about to go to India with the ATS; she is wondering if Peter, her boyfriend of several years, will join her there and whether he will propose to her.

The most extraordinary tale is that of Henry Beckingham. He survived the entire conflict working in bomb disposal, and by May 1945 was in charge of clearing mines in the Channel Islands, where he remained until 1946. He ended his military career as a captain and was last heard of enjoying a long retirement, having published several books.

APPENDIX

AIR RAID CASUALTIES

146,777 civilians were killed, missing believed killed or seriously injured, subdivided as follows:
Men: 67,661 Women: 63,221
Children under 16: 15,358 Unidentified: 537

Civil defence workers on duty (the General Services and the Regular and Auxiliary Police and Fire Services) suffered 6,838 casualties (2,379 killed and 4,459 seriously injured), which are included in the previous total. Of these, 6,220 were men and 618 women.

The proportion of casualties attributed to the enemy's chief weapons has been estimated as follows:

	Killed	Seriously Injured	Total
Bombs	51,509	61,423	112,932
Flying bombs	6,184	17,981	24,165
Long-range rockets	2,754	6,523	9,277
Cross-Channel bombardment	148	255	403
Total	60,595	86,182	146,777

London suffered over 80,000 of the estimated total for the country of 146,777 fatal and serious casualties. Outside London, only Birmingham and Liverpool suffered more than 5,000 such casualties.

Major bombardments (attacks in which more than 100 tons of HE bombs were successfully aimed at the target):

London	71
Birmingham	8
Liverpool, Birkenhead	8
Plymouth-Devonport	8
Bristol-Avonmouth	6
Glasgow-Clydeside	5
Southampton	4
Hull	3
Manchester	3
Portsmouth	3
Belfast	2
Coventry	2
Cardiff	1
Newcastle-Tyneside	1
Nottingham	1
Sheffield	1

FLYING BOMB AND LONG-RANGE ROCKET INCIDENTS BY COUNTY

Counties	**Flying Bombs**	**Long-Range Rockets**
London (region)	2,420	517
Kent	1,444	64
Sussex	886	4
Essex	412	378
Surrey	295	8
Suffolk	93	13
Hertfordshire	82	34
Hampshire	80	–
Buckinghamshire	27	2
Norfolk	13	29
Berkshire	12	1
Bedfordshire	10	3
Lancashire	8	–
Yorkshire	7	–
Cheshire	6	–
Cambridgeshire	5	1
Northamptonshire	4	–
Oxfordshire	4	–
Isle of Ely	3	–
Derbyshire	3	–
Huntingdonshire	2	–
Lincolnshire	2	–
Durham	1	–
Nottinghamshire	1	–
Leicestershire	1	–
Rutland	1	–
Shropshire	1	–
Total	**5,823***	**1,054†**

* London Region received 41 per cent of flying bombs and 49 per cent of long-range rockets; † 271 of these flying bombs and 4 of the long-range rockets fell in the sea. From: Civil Defence T.H. O'Brian

ACKNOWLEDGEMENTS

I am grateful to many people who have helped me with personal memories and diaries during my research for this project, and especially those in family history and local history societies who helped publicise my request for information on websites, in newsletters and journals.

I must also thank Sophie Bradshaw, and Abigail Wood and Christine McMorris from The History Press, and the staff of the Imperial War Museum.

Thanks too to William and Ralph Harris-Brown for their administrative support, Mike Brown for invaluable help and advice, and, as ever, all three for their patience.

I am grateful to the following for their kind permission in allowing me to quote from original material: Gill Ankers for the letter of her mother, Kathleen Hanlon; Fiona Godlee, editor of the *British Medical Journal*, for permission to reproduce the letter from Dr Duncan Leys and extracts from papers by Robert Lee and F. Wilfred Willway; Glasgow City Council archives for memories of James Hastings and Tryphena Nixon.

Thanks also go to the Imperial War Museum, individual contributors and their families for the use of the following original documents: J.G. Atherton, H.W. Atterbury, C.M. Baker, Henry Beckingham, Elizabeth Belsey, John Belsey, C. Brownbill, Betty Bullard, Margaret Chifney, Phillip Chignell, Roy Clevely, H.R. Clothier, Betty Holbrook, Kenneth Holmes,

Constance Logan-Wright, Claire Lowry, Tom King, Anne Lee Michell, R.H. Lloyd-Jones, Hetty Long, Ann Maxtone Graham, Lily Pearson, Joyce Pomorska, Choc Steed, J.L. Stevens, Don Thompson, Jeanne and Marion Thompson, Rose Uttin and Mollie Wilson. I am grateful to Graeme Kirkwood, historian for Strathclyde fire services, for the report by A.S. Pratten; Jim Purdey for his private memoir; West Glamorgan Archive Service for permission to quote from the diary of Basil Radford; the Museum of London for permission to reproduce the letter from Will, ARP warden in Leytonstone, and Bob Boyd.

Books and Pamphlets:

Bob Boyd, Bromley U3As, *The Day War Broke Out*, 1995

Cecil Beaton, Diaries (1939–45), *The Years Between*, Weidenfeld & Nicolson, 1965

Eric Wilton, *Centre Crew: A Memory of the Royal Observer Corps*, published privately for members of 'B' Crew of the Royal Observer Corps Centre at Bromley, Kent, 1946

James Doherty, *Post 381*, Friar's Bush Press, 1989

Mike Brown, *Put That Light Out*, Sutton, 1999

Muriel Simkin, *Voices From the Past: The Blitz*, ed. John Simkin, Spartacus, 1987

N.W. Hardy, *Eastbourne 1939–45: A complete record of nearly six years of war in Eastbourne*, Strange the Printer Ltd, 1945

Phil Piratin, *Our Flag Stays Red*, Thames Publications, 1948, loan courtesy of Frank Chalmers

Quentin Reynolds, *The Wounded Don't Cry*, E.P. Dutton, 1941

Reginald Bell, *The London Bullseye*, Cassell and Co., 1943

W.L. Richards, *Pembrokeshire Under Fire – the story of the Air Raids of 1940–41*, J.W. Hammond and Co. Ltd, 1965